iz Miller has really done some
Skating gives the reader a tast
a pair of in-line skates can pro\

—*Kris Simeone, Inline Certification P*
International Inline Skating Associa.

iz Miller's passion for the sport of in-line skating comes across
clearly in *Advanced In-Line Skating*. This is the most complete
resource for skaters of all abilities and includes all they need
to reach their next level. Liz leaves no gray areas in explaining
even the smallest details of every in-line discipline with factual,
up-to-date information and resources. I recommend this book to
everyone, even beginners, for a comprehensive overview of
in-line skating."

—*Suzanne Nottingham, Examiner, IISA Instructor Certification Program,*
coauthor of Fitness In-Line Skating

his book cracks open the world of in-line skating for those
looking for more than straight-line skating on their local bike
path. As people look for innovative ways to reduce stress, have
fun, and get and stay fit, *Advanced In-Line Skating* delivers a
timely guide to getting the most from a pair of skates."

—*Adam Steer, Director, In-Line Certification Program, Canada*

his book is the next logical step after *Get Rolling*. It's brimming
with well-written, advanced skating techniques and key exercises
to help transform you into the skater you want to be. It covers
everything from speedskating, roller hockey, aggressive, downhill,
hybrid sports to essential safety tips, shopping advice, definitions
of skate terminology and just improving and sharpening your
rolling-around skills. Pack this book (with your helmet) in your
skate bag and take it with you to the trail, road, or rink. It rocks
and so will you!"

—*Jim Fink, Seattle Skate Patrol*

Advanced In-Line Skating

ADVANCED IN-LINE SKATING

■ LIZ MILLER ■

RAGGED MOUNTAIN PRESS / McGRAW-HILL

CAMDEN, MAINE • NEW YORK • SAN FRANCISCO • WASHINGTON, D.C. • AUCKLAND
BOGOTÁ • CARACAS • LISBON • LONDON • MADRID • MEXICO CITY • MILAN • MONTREAL
NEW DELHI • SAN JUAN • SINGAPORE • SYDNEY • TOKYO • TORONTO

Ragged Mountain Press
A Division of The McGraw-Hill Companies

10 9 8 7 6 5 4 3 2 1

Library of Congress Cataloging-in-Publication Data
Miller, Liz.
 Advanced in-line skating / by Liz Miller.
  p. cm.
 Includes bibliographical references and index.
 ISBN 0-07-135448-4
  1. In-line skating—Handbooks, manuals, etc.
 I. Title: Advanced in-line skating. II. Title.

GV859.73.M548 2000
796.21—dc21   99-086503

Questions regarding the content of this book should be addressed to
Ragged Mountain Press
P.O. Box 220
Camden, ME 04843
www.raggedmountainpress.com

Questions regarding the ordering of this book should be addressed to
The McGraw-Hill Companies
Customer Service Department
P.O. Box 547
Blacklick, OH 43004
Retail customers: 1-800-262-4729
Bookstores: 1-800-722-4726

This book is printed on 70-lb. Citation
Printed by Quebecor Printing, Fairfield, PA
Design by Shannon Thomas
Illustrations by Michael Gellatly
Production management by Dan Kirchoff
Edited by Tom McCarthy and Kate Thompson

Dr. Scholl's, Gatorade, Gym Skate, Jazzercize, Kevlar, Lycra, PIC, Rollerblade, Runners Lube, SkidSkins, Spandex, Styrofoam, Thorlo, and Velcro are registered trademarks.

"Roll Model" on page 2 is excerpted by permission from SkateCentral.com, <www.snapsite.com/guests/ sk8ctrl/public/custom/citysports/inline.adventures.html>

■ CONTENTS ■

■ PREFACE ■

At the conclusion of my instructional clinics, I am frequently asked, "So after I get good at this, what's next?" *Advanced In-Line Skating* answers that question for my past students and for all skaters who have conquered the basics and are eager to see where their wheels can take them next.

As your enthusiastic guide, I introduce the turn of the millennium's most popular skating pursuits and make sure entry-level participants will find enough detail for a safe and informed start. For the competitive disciplines, where my own near-decade of experience falls short, I've enlisted the help of known experts who have contributed to and validated the information in those chapters and can serve as "roll models" to inspire your efforts. It is my hope that each reader finds at least one chapter that excites a hunger to train, tour, or test his or her limits by trying something new on skates.

Who knows, perhaps one of you will invent the next in-line rage!

■ ACKNOWLEDGMENTS ■

I'm grateful to have Dan Kibler as my webmaster, editor, photographer, favorite skate and ski buddy, voice of reason, ball tosser for Whitney the cat, and life partner.

A squad of experts contributed their time and expertise to make sure this book presents accurate and timely information to guide people safely toward advanced skating. Thanks to Eddy Matzger, Suzan Davis, Suzanne Nottingham, Allan Wright, Adam Steer, Jo Ann Schneider Farris, Richard Humphrey, Robert Schmunk, Kris Simeone, Anna Stubbs, Barrie Hartman, Bobby Hull Jr., Bettina Bigelow, Steve MacDonald, Scott Peer, Zack Phillips, Peter Marcus, and Tom LaGarde. I'm also grateful to the industry contacts who supplied leads, product information, or photographs, including Gene Kliot of Transpack, Larry Newman of Miller Sports, Brian Levine of Parabolics, Craig Zelinske of Salomon, Rick Dobrowski of Mission Hockey, Reggie Winner of *California Hockey & Skating Magazine*, Steven F. Betterly of Riedell Shoes Inc., Justin Anderson, and the Wisconsin Pharmacal Company. I'm in debt to Lester Leong, a fellow IISA-certified instructor, for being such a willing and photogenic skills demonstrator.

Thanks very much to my friends Molly Mulhern, Dan Kirchoff, and Tom McCarthy at Ragged Mountain Press, who made giving birth to a book seem much easier than it really was.

∎ INTRODUCTION ∎

As a self-appointed in-line missionary, it is my constant (and irresistible) desire to enlighten the growing ranks of skaters across the globe to the ever-widening world of rolling opportunities and inspire them to experience in-line skating to its fullest. There is so much you can do with wheels attached to your feet! By picking up this book, you've already acknowledged that you're ready to advance beyond the basics to the next, more adventurous level of skating.

The Advanced Skater

Among the millions of people who are now frequent in-line participants, those who are truly competent rise above the crowd. He's the guy at the city park whose dancing skate frames glint in the sunlight as he spins, moonwalks, and prances to a boom box, never losing balance or missing a beat. She's the skater in a tuck who passes cyclists so effortlessly on the bike path, her slow, graceful strokes belying the powered push that makes her whiz by. He's the fellow with a day pack often seen either scooting to and from work or running rolling errands downtown.

More likely than not, the skaters who stand out from the crowd have adopted an in-line lifestyle. They've totally incorporated the sport's convenience, social opportunities, and health benefits into their daily lives. Going beyond the essential basics, they've acquired an advanced sense of balance, elegant coordination, and the physical confidence that is so evident to those who observe them. What is it that makes these skaters different? Nothing more than their passion for skating plus many hours spent at a roll.

Eddy Matzger—winning endurance competitor and most likely the world's best-known skating goodwill ambassador—is my idea of a total skater. He's not just "advanced" skill-wise, he's fully ensconced in the lifestyle. He'll go anywhere on skates, including a climb up Mount Kilimanjaro, and once confessed he probably spends more time on skates than off. But what impresses me the most is his insatiable desire to share his love and knowledge of skating with people all over the world at all ability levels.

Venturing Out

Approximately 90 percent of the world's in-line skaters are recreational participants, skating primarily for pleasure and social opportunities, usually on sidewalks and auto-free bike paths. But

ROLL MODEL

Thanks to my Dutch grandmother, my unlikely career began. I went to Holland to celebrate her 80th birthday in 1988, and saw by chance an in-line race in progress. When a cluster of brightly colored skaters came screaming around the corner at breakneck speeds, I was immediately smitten. I canceled my ticket home and stayed on to buy skates and practice hurriedly for my first race a week later, where I got lapped by people three times my age.

Oma was one of my biggest skate spon-

Eddy Matzger, a total skater.

sors, a true patron of the sport. I stayed with her in Amsterdam during the winters of '91, '92, and '93, as well as many summers when I raced on in-lines. Oma wasn't much interested in sports, but she took a fancy to skating and always clipped articles out of the newspaper and sent them to me.

It wasn't until 1994, after being humbled repeatedly and nearly giving up many times along the way, that I finally cracked one wide open and won my first race in Holten. Oma was asleep when I returned late that evening, but she knew the outcome first thing in the morning when she saw and smelled the huge bouquet of flowers sitting on the table. Oma was a landscape painter who loved to paint flowers, and those flowers live on in her oils. Since my memories of my Oma and skating are inseparably intertwined, she'll live as long as I skate—in other words, she'll live forever.

—Eddy Matzger, in-line adventurer, world-record speedskater,
and founder-instructor of the Eddy Matzger Workshop Weekend Skate Clinics

Salomon North America

any skater who sticks with just one favorite in-line discipline will never attain a truly advanced level of skill and will miss out on a rich in-line lifestyle.

If you are ready to embrace advanced in-line skating, you have only to decide how you'd like to grow. Explore all the possibilities and expand your paved paradise at the same time. The variety of skating opportunities is growing almost as fast as the sport's popularity. Each of the following summaries has its own chapter in this book to guide newcomers safely toward complete participation.

Fitness, Endurance, and Cross Training

In-line workouts are ideal for those who are interested in building and maintaining healthy bodies through sustained physical effort. The low-impact in-line stride delivers cardiovascular, body-composition, and muscular benefits. Participation in recreational in-line marathons, mileage-based fundraisers, and other endurance events are a natural progression for skaters who enjoy the benefits of such training.

Touring

Satisfy the wanderlust within by exploring your region's business parks, ritzy neighborhood hills, or roadside bike routes. You'll find excellent fitness benefits and sightseeing opportunities on long, uninterrupted rail-trails or bike routes not just close to home but in exotic destinations the world over. A guided skate tour in the Netherlands, France, or Switzerland is a wonderful chance to experience a new culture in a unique way or to begin new friendships that can last a lifetime.

Skate-to-Ski

Skaters have learned they can combine gravity with asphalt and carving skills to improve their technique and enjoyment on snowy ski slopes. The Professional Ski Instructors Association (PSIA) uses in-line drills for dry-land performance training to improve their alpine skiing technique. For both alpine and cross-country skiers, those who train on in-lines with ski poles not only become more centered over their skis and in better control of their edges, they also learn how to manage both climbing and descending steeper asphalt hills.

Freestyle

Freestyle includes everything from casual or competitive dancing to the funky beat of a boom box to running a cones course to performance figure skating. In 1997, in-lines specifically designed for office figure skating first appeared on the market, complete with leather boots and a rolling front-mounted stopper that emulated the toe pick. This innovation spurred the adaptation of figure skating jumps and spins to in-line.

Speed Skating

For competitive souls who love speed, racing is the natural next stroke. In-line speed skating entered the 1990s on the urethane wheels of roller skate (now referred to as "quads") converts. Many race promoters include non-pro divisions, providing interested amateurs a taste of the race. Events for outdoor and indoor track races are growing in number every year.

Roller Hockey

The excitement of team dynamics, stick handling, and competitive play quickly improves striding and maneuvering skills, because hockey players have to think *on* their feet instead of *about* their feet. Roller hockey at both the pro and amateur levels is growing as fast as new rinks can be built.

Aggressive

If you're drawn by "X-treme" sports and still believe in your own immortality, consider the thrills of launching off a ramp or half-pipe to do aerial stunts or tackling the urban landscape by sliding across concrete edges and down stair railings. Besides specialized skates and courage, aggressive skating demands precise footwork, excellent balance, and more than a little endurance, in every sense of the word.

Downhill

To most in-liners, a successful downhill experience means getting to the bottom without crashing or accelerating out of control. Hill courses set up with cones or gates attract a small but growing cadre of skaters who continue to hone the technical aspects of fast downhill slalom runs. And in Europe, wildly enthusiastic audiences greet heavily padded downhillers seeking maximum speed on mountain road courses. Opportunities to train and compete in these two disciplines are expanding as this group of specialists and its audience appeal grows.

Hybrid Sports and Activities

Since the early natural adaptation of roller hockey, a variety of other in-line sports have emerged, some quite surprising.

- In the last three years, separate organizing bodies have brought soccer and basketball to wheels, and more than one version of roller derby has been reincarnated on television.

- Wind sailing on large, breezy parking lots brings dry-land thrills to novice and experienced skate-sailors alike.

- Off-road-style skates with knobby, air-filled wheels are opening up some ski areas during the off-season.

How to Use This Book

To get the most from *Advanced In-Line Skating* you should already be a competent intermediate skater. If you have never taken a lesson from a certified in-line skating instructor, it would be wise to pick up a copy of my first book, *Get Rolling: The Beginner's Guide to In-Line Skating*. The beginning and intermediate skills detailed in its step-by-step instructions are components for many of the advanced moves described in these pages. You'll find descriptions of the essential skills for each experience level in chapter 2.

Advanced In-Line Skating is the ideal roadmap to new adventures on in-line skates, no matter which route you choose. Along with a brief history, required gear, and a list of key skills, all chapters except chapter 1 include a Dialect section where you'll find definitions of commonly used terms. Roll Model sidebars include personal stories or enlightening information offered by recognized experts. Resources at the end of each chapter point you to more information about related organizations, publications, Web sites, and instructional help.

Part 1, The Skating Lifestyle, introduces lifestyle activities to be enjoyed by the avid skater and the gear and skills that support them. If you are one of the skating majority who is not interested in competitive activities, read part 1 in chapter sequence for a logical progression in abilities and experience guaranteed to expand your skating horizons. On the way you'll learn how to skate farther and faster with less work and discover a world of new opportunities for adventure and friendship.

Chapter 1, Equipping Your Sports Closet, describes skate gear and accessories, how to maintain your equipment, the skaters' first-aid kit (along with advice for treating road rash), and the nice-to-have items that make a day of skating easier and more fun.

In chapter 2, Key Skills for the Advanced Skater, you'll review the beginning and intermediate skills that every advanced skater should possess, including step-by-step instructions for a powerful and efficient stride. Here you'll read about both uphill and downhill techniques and discover a bag o' tricks that develop balance, agility, and coordination.

You'll learn the best ways to build aerobic and muscular endurance and decrease body fat in chapter 3; plus you'll find tips for how to avoid injury through warm-ups, stretching, and cool-down; map your own fitness skating program; and use

other sports for cross training to improve your in-line performance.

Chapter 4, In-Line Touring, introduces the concept of route exploration on in-lines, including how to properly prepare for adventure-filled skating jaunts. Find out how to plan for everything from a day trip to a city's Friday Night Skate to a weeklong guided tour in another state or country.

Chapter 5, Skate-to-Ski, is a gift to alpine ski enthusiasts. This chapter describes proper slalom form and then moves on to a series of progressive drills that will make your first day back on skis a magical experience.

In chapter 6, Freestyle, you'll learn about street dance, figure skating, and slaloming through a row of cones. You'll get to know the lingo; practice some popular dance, slalom, and artistic moves; and read about opportunities for formal competition.

Part 2, A Competitive Start, is for people eager to move beyond lifestyle skating to more extreme or competitive pursuits. You'll find the gear, key skills, terminology, and other entry-level information that will prepare you to safely and knowledgeably join others who can help speed your progress. Where noted, skills, training methods, or entire chapters from part 1 are prerequisites.

Discover speed skate components, technique, race formats, and how to prepare for a race in chapter 7, Speed Skating. The Speed Skating Resources section lists the organizations, publications, and workshops racers depend on to gain a competitive edge.

Chapter 8, Roller Hockey, presents all you need to know about gearing up, basic rules of the game, where to learn key footwork and stick handling skills, a glossary of roller hockey terms and moves, and how to find a team or league to play with.

In chapter 9, Aggressive Skating, you'll enter the world of street and ramp skating. Here you'll find tips about the gear, a translation of some trick names, starter skills, and the most popular sources for learning tricks both online and in print.

Chapter 10, Technical Downhill, describes

the techniques of harnessing speed for maximum performance on steep slalom runs. Learn about the courses, the races, survival skills, special gear, and gate training.

Want to put your newly honed skills to work on the playing field? You'll find out how in chapter 11, Hybrid Team Sports. Roller soccer requires agility, finesse, and a few like-minded friends; this chapter provides the sport history, basic rules, court layout, gear, and terms you need to get a new team rolling. The section on roller basketball gives hoops addicts the skinny on organizing teams for participation in a league game, including skate-specific rules, prerequisite skills, and court requirements.

▪ PART ONE ▪

THE SKATING
LIFESTYLE

Dan Kibler

■ CHAPTER ONE ■

EQUIPPING YOUR SPORTS CLOSET

DIALECT

ABEC system: A bearing precision rating system developed by the Annular Bearing Engineering Council: an ABEC 5 bearing is manufactured more precisely than an ABEC 1 and can provide a smoother, faster ride.

axle guide: A small (and easily lost!) metal or plastic disk that fits into the holes on both sides of the skate frame, held in place by the spacers and bolts. In some skate models, the axle guides can be rotated 180 degrees, which makes it possible to shift a wheel's position in relation to the frame (for example, to "rocker" the center wheels or lengthen the wheel base).

bearings: The hardware that makes a smooth-spinning wheel (two per wheel), using small ball bearings that roll in a track called the race.

bolts: Various bolt configurations attach wheels to the skate frame. Virtually all are configured for installation with an Allen wrench.

(continued on next page)

Expanding your in-line horizons means acquiring an equally expanding collection of specialty skates accessories, clothes, tools, wheels, and gotta-have-it gadgets.

Shopping for Skates

To pursue any advanced in-line activity successfully, it's best to upgrade to a skate model specifically designed for that discipline. You'll find specific equipment advice for the various types of skating in the Gear sections of the chapters that follow.

Although specialty skates invariably force you to dig deeper into your savings account, remember that when purchasing any type of technical gear, you get exactly what you pay for. Go ahead and look for year-end sales or used skates, but do *not* try to save money by buying at the bottom of the manufacturer's line. A low price guarantees low-quality materials and probable foot pain, poor stability, slow bearings, and a short useful life for the skates. See the Recommended Skate Manufacturers section at the end of this chapter.

When purchasing new skates, remember

- Shop at a skate specialty shop to find the best selection and qualified sales staff. These folks sell only from reputable manufacturers and can help you choose the right skate for you. If you have a choice of outlets, stop in for a visit at each to compare customer service, selection, and prices.

- Don't shop by catalog or order skates on the Internet unless you know exactly what you'll be getting and, preferably, have had a chance to demo the skates you want to buy.

DIALECT *(continued from previous page)*

canting: A boot adjustment that affects lateral tilt.

chassis: Another name for the in-line skate frame into which wheels are installed.

coned: The shaved-off state of a wheel that is worn on one side, indicating the wheel needs to be replaced or flipped over and rotated.

cuff: The portion of the in-line skate that encases the ankle.

diameter: The measurement that determines wheel sizes; usually marked on the side of the wheel in millimeters.

durometer: A rating system used to classify in-line wheel hardness; usually printed on the side of the wheel with a two-digit number (in the range of 75–100+) followed by the letter A. The higher the number, the harder the wheel.

footbed: The replaceable insole of the skate boot.

frame: The chassis attached to the sole of the in-line boot into which the wheels are bolted (custom frames can be purchased for some skate boots).

hub (core): A material that the wheel's polyurethane bonds to, providing torsional stability and a solid seat for the bearings.

polyurethane: The plastic material used to manufacture most in-line wheels.

profile: The wheel's shape when viewed from the edge. Wide profiles result in quick-turning, slower skates; wheels with the narrowest profile are used for speed.

race: The track inside a bearing around which the balls roll.

rotating: Flipping the wheels and swapping their positions to make sure they wear evenly and last longer.

shield: The exterior cover on either side of a bearing. In "serviceable" bearings, these are removable to allow easier cleaning.

spacers: The metal or plastic tube that sits within a wheel to stabilize the bearings.

● Spend as much money as you can afford—you are investing in a quality performance tool that needs to be comfortable for hour upon hour and, in some sports, give you a competitive edge. A good pair of fitness or aggressive skates lists for around $300, the best hockey skates run $500, and custom speed skates can cost anywhere from $600 to $1,500.

● When trying on skates, wear the socks you plan to use with them. They should be designed specifically for athletic activity, so they will wick moisture away from your foot and prevent blisters. Choose thin rather than bulky socks so they won't bunch up inside the boot.

● Women's skate models are available from the better manufacturers. These usually compensate for a woman's lower calf muscle and narrower Achilles tendon. If the tag doesn't differentiate genders, the skate is unisex.

● Seek a comfortable boot, but make sure you purchase a snug-fitting skate that delivers the required precision for your planned activity. After a few miles of skating, a skate that fits too loose (but was really comfy in the shop!) will soon feel sloppy and cause blisters.

If you can't afford new skates, with most brands you can still modify the wheels and bearings to meet specialized needs. Better brands of recreational skates will accommodate the faster bearings and taller, harder wheels used by speed skaters or wheels specifically designed for hockey or aggressive skating. For sport-specific advice, see the Gear sections of the later chapters.

In the Store

Wear the skates you want to buy for 15 minutes or longer to give them a chance to hurt. Before you commit to the purchase, you should be satisfied that

- the overall fit is snug, but you can wiggle your toes.

- with straight knees, your toes lightly touch the end of the boot.

- when you bend your knees and press your shins forward (a normal skating stance), your toes no longer touch and your heels remain snugly cupped by the boot.

- both skates remain perfectly upright when you stand in a natural, shoulder-width skating stance.

- there are no noticeable pressure points across the top of either arch, at the widest part of your feet, or along the fronts of your shin bones.

- the insoles feel comfortable and support-ive underfoot (or can be replaced with your own).

- when you assume a speed skating tuck, the front of the boot flexes with your foot without undue pressure across the tops of the toes.

Customizing the Fit

Nonplastic boots used by hockey, fitness, and speed skaters often need some fine-tuning to prevent pain or blisters. The sales personnel at most skate shops can heat-mold leather, synthetic leather, and the materials used in most high-end skates to match the shape of your foot. It takes about half an hour to heat the boots, lace and buckle them up tightly, and then wear them as you wait for the material to cool down in the new shape. You can also use a blow dryer at home for further reshaping.

It's especially important to correct a skate that is constantly tipped onto the inside or out-side edge. Pronounced tipping to the inside is referred to as **pronation**; a tip to the outside is called **supination** (a slight supination is preferred by some speed skaters). If you cannot fix the tilt by tightening the top buckle of your skates, attack the problem from the inside by adding a partial insert under the insole or swapping to a different

footbed. Some plastic boot fitness skates have a canting feature that lets you adjust the skate's cuff by turning a screw to tip it left or right over the boot. If necessary, see your local ski-boot fitter for help.

Fitness and speed skates usually have a mov-able frame that can be shifted to the left or right in order to correct tipping or facilitate the outside-edge set-down.

Shopping for Kids' Skates

Don't waste money on the cheap, limited selection of kids' skates typically sold at big chain sporting-goods, department, and toy stores. These not only wear out early, they often retard the skater's devel-opment because of a painful fit, bad ankle support, and slow-rolling wheels.

To outfit a child with in-lines, purchase one of the youth skate models sold in specialty shops. These will accommodate up to four foot sizes, us-ing either a stretchy boot liner, two different-sized liners, or an extendable sole. The price is usually $75 to $100, and it's well worth gaining a longer useful skate life.

Equipment Maintenance

Boots and Brakes

After skating, air-dry your skates in a well-ventilated area to reduce the bacteria buildup that results in smelly boots. Secure the tongue as though your foot is in the boot to make sure it dries without forming a crimp. Replace the heel brake before it wears down to the screw head or metal core. (Many brands have a wear limit line molded into the rubber.) Buy two or three brakes at a time, because even good skate shops have a hard time stocking parts for every type of skate they've ever sold.

Wheels

Periodically rotate your wheels to even out the wear so they'll last longer. This not only saves a few bucks but also gives you a smoother, safer ride. For some types of skaters, skating, and wheel types, even with frequent rotation a set of wheels might last only a few weeks. That's why it's important to watch for shaved-off edges, which indicate the need for prompt maintenance. For example, a skater on soft wheels might experience coning after a single day of skate-to-ski training. And speed skaters install new wheels before every race to ensure the least amount of drag from road contact.

There are two steps involved in wheel maintenance: flipping each wheel so the flattened side faces the opposite direction (usually away from the inside arch) and rotating the wheel positions. Swap the wheels with the most wear with those show-ing less wear. Swap wheels between the right and left skate as needed. Use a clean rag to gently wipe away the grit from each bearing surface, taking care not to grind the dust inside.

While you've got the wheels out of the frames, wipe down the boot and wheel frame and clear the frame of any debris that might be lodged inside.

When it's time to replace your wheels, be sure to purchase the proper size for your frame and the wheel profile that most suits your type of skating (see figure below left).

Bearings

Even if you avoid puddles and sand, dirt and moisture have a way of filtering into your bearings and slowing you down. Cheaper bearings are usually not serviceable because their shields are not designed to be removed. Clean the outsides of non-serviceable bearings by wiping them with a dry cloth. To convert these for frequent maintenance, use a tiny, sharp object to pry off one of the fixed metal shields and discard it. After cleaning, install the open side of the bearing toward the inside of the wheel to keep out dirt.

Profile	Size in Millimeters	Hardness in Durometer
Race	76-82 mm	76-90 A
Fitness	72-82 mm	78-82 A
Recreation	72-76 mm	78-82 A
Hockey	60-76 mm	75-90 A
Aggressive	43-72 mm	82-101 A

Wheel types.

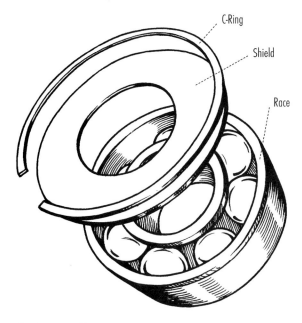

C-Ring

Shield

Race

Bearing assembly.

Clean and lubricate serviceable bearings immediately after they get wet or whenever you begin to notice drag, unusual vibrations, or squeaking.

1. Remove the wheels from the skates and extract both bearings out of each wheel. (Bearing pushers are described on page 18.)

2. Remove one shield from each of the bearings. With luck, this will be as easy as peeling back a little rubber ring to expose the balls and inner race. Metal shields are usually held in place with tiny C-rings, which must be pried out from under the edge of the bearing case. Use a pushpin to pull out the exposed end of the C and pop it out. Once you've removed the ring, you can pry off the shield. (If it's stuck, try easing it off with the pushpin or soaking it in solvent for a few minutes and then tapping the bearing on a hard surface.) Leave the balls and cage installed.

3. Collect all shields, C-rings, and the open bearings in a container just deep enough that these parts can be submersed in solvent. Place the bearings open-side down so the dirt can drop out as it dissolves. Add your favorite solvent:

   - full-strength biodegradable detergent, or
   - citrus solvent, or
   - nail polish remover (flammable and smelly!). Avoid highly flammable solvents such as lacquer thinner and gasoline.

4. Swirl the bearings in the container and probe with a soft toothbrush if necessary to remove dirt and grease. Soak really gritty bearings overnight.

5. Rinse the bearings with clean solvent or, to remove all traces of solvent, use hot soapy water (but expect a longer drying time).

6. Air-dry or blow-dry thoroughly.

7. Relubricate with just enough of your favorite grease or oil to coat the balls and race, using

   - 3 to 4 drops of sewing machine or other household oil (spins slightly faster than grease but attracts grit and requires more frequent maintenance), or
   - grease (might take a few miles to expel residue and spin freely but lasts longer).

8. Reassemble bearings, wheels, and skates.

Protection

Experience versus Injuries

It would be irresponsible for me to suggest that the better your skills and the longer you've been skating, the less likely it is you'll get hurt. In fact, the exact opposite was proven to be true in a study published in the February 1999 issue of the *American Journal of Public Health*. Why? Because as you increase the number of hours you skate, the variety of moves you perform, and the types of terrain you skate on, the odds for injury go up.

The study reported that the most common injuries (26 percent) were related to collisions or trying to avoid them. Attempting to perform tricks on ramps, rails, or ledges also caused a significant number of injuries (21 percent), as did frequent weekly skating sessions. The injury rate was four times higher in the group that skated more than ten hours a week than for those who said they skated only one or two hours. In 1996, the Consumer Product Safety Commission (CPSC) stated that up to one-third of all in-line injuries requiring a trip to the emergency room could be prevented or lessened in severity by wearing wrist guards.

While the above statistics are sobering, in-line injury protection is a matter of choice, not chance. You can't anticipate every surprise that skating in the real world will toss beneath your wheels, but you *can* control your odds for an injury-free outcome. Get qualified instruction or coaching to learn the basics, wear proper protective gear each time you go out, and skate within your true abilities.

You'll notice that each chapter's Gear section recommends you wear a helmet and pads, regardless of discipline. This is how you take control of your own risk of injury. Skate safely as you explore your wheeled heart's desires, and you'll have fun through a ripe old age!

Helmet Primer

Unlike many other bones in your body, a fractured skull can lead to severe consequences. Science has discovered that concussions can have lasting effects on brain function. Even when all other organs are healthy and strong, without a working brain you are "brain dead." Don't wait for your own brush with mortality or the death of a bareheaded skating buddy before you finally decide you need to protect your head. My unprotected skate pal died the same day I'd donned a helmet for the first time—close enough to convince me.

There is no excuse to leave your helmet behind. No matter how awesome you are as a skater, you will never be in control of the unpredictable people, animals, and environment surrounding you. For example, think about all those motorists chatting on their cell phones as you wait to cross the street or skate alongside in a bike lane. Your helmet sends a distinct visual signal to half-absent drivers that you are moving much faster than a pedestrian, reducing your chances of being cut off or run over at a corner.

FEATURES

Bicycle helmets are the most commonly used head protection for recreational in-line skating. They work just fine, although some manufacturers do offer helmets for skating that provide more coverage for the back of the head. You can read about special helmets for other in-line disciplines in their respective chapters.

When purchasing a new helmet, look for the CPSC sticker inside. In 1999, the Consumer Product Safety Commission decreed that all helmets must comply with their federal safety standards for impact resistance, strap strength, and "roll off" during an accident. The CPSC rating now supersedes stickers proving ANSI, Snell, or ASTM compliance. Replace your helmets after five or more years; sweat, sun, and heat cause deterioration to the protective materials.

Besides the CPSC-specified safety features, a helmet might offer increased coverage for the back of the head, a built-in or detachable visor, internal reinforcement, a rear stabilizer, a custom-fit liner, lightweight materials, a multiple- or directed-vent cooling system, hinged strap adjusters, and an aerodynamic shape. Multifeatured models run from $30 to $80, though top-of-the-line racing helmets can be as high as $150.

PROPER HELMET FIT

Make sure your lid fits well and is adjusted properly; a helmet's impact protection capabilities are useless if it doesn't stay in place.

- Use the manufacturer's foam inserts to get a snug fit.

- When properly adjusted, all straps should lie flat against your head.

- Situate the joints where the front and rear straps meet so they form a V directly below your earlobes to prevent shifting from side to side.

Dan Kibler

Not one helmet in sight!

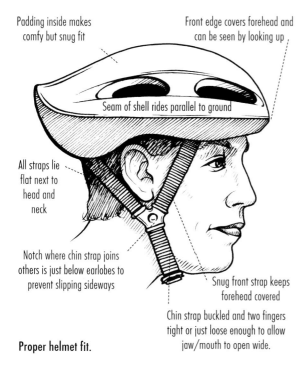

Padding inside makes comfy but snug fit

Front edge covers forehead and can be seen by looking up

Seam of shell rides parallel to ground

All straps lie flat next to head and neck

Notch where chin strap joins others is just below earlobes to prevent slipping sideways

Snug front strap keeps forehead covered

Chin strap buckled and two fingers tight or just loose enough to allow jaw/mouth to open wide.

Proper helmet fit.

- Adjust the chin strap so you cannot pull the helmet off your head. You should be able to feel the strap pressing under your jaw when you open your mouth wide and just see the front rim at the top of your peripheral vision.

- If the front of the helmet slips up and exposes your forehead (your brain!), shorten the two front straps. Position the helmet so the horizontal seam between shell and Styrofoam (if any) rides parallel to the ground.

Protective Pads

Shop at a store where you can try on gear before buying it to make sure it doesn't bind uncomfortably.

Wrist guards with a splint on both sides and a hard plastic surface prevent scraped palms and broken or fractured wrists. Look for breathable mesh on the sides to keep hands cool or articulated hinges at the wrists to allow freer wrist movement. See the Gear sections of the chapters 8 and 9 to read about wrist protection specially designed for roller hockey and aggressive skating.

Buy **elbow** and **knee pads** sturdy enough to prevent bruises from full-body-weight landings during a high-speed crash. These are your first line of defense when a meeting with the pavement is imminent; sometimes they represent the only way out of a bad situation. The hard plastic will slide to deflect some of the impact, but only if the pad stays firmly fixed over your knee or elbow. Slip-on pads (with knit sleeves) are much more likely to stay in place than those that just wrap on with Velcro.

Lightweight or heavy-duty **padded shorts** give skaters confidence along with extra protection for the pelvis bones when doing downhill training, racing, or aerial tricks. (Beginners like them, too.) For almost invisible protection, you can buy padded bike-style shorts (and other outfits) made of abrasion-resistant material (see Gear Resources, pages 19–20). Other options range from individual foam pads you can insert in your clothes, to stretchy shorts with removable tailbone and hip padding, to belt-on tailbone protection. You usually can wear these under other baggy clothing.

Outfitting Your Child

Children are especially injury-prone but, unfortunately, are usually unaware they're in a dangerous situation until it's too late. Make sure the helmet and pads you buy for your kids are comfortable and fit properly, as described above. Kids will resist wearing pads with straps that itch or bind.

When parents don't wear gear, kids believe that when they get big they won't need it either. This is an opportunity to ensure a lifelong helmet habit that will protect your child well into the future.

First-Aid Supplies and Treatments

A well-stocked skating first-aid kit includes

- moleskin and mini scissors
- bandages of various sizes
- sterile gauze pads and medical tape
- Second Skin or similar membrane product

A skater's first-aid kit.

- stick-on bunion rings (for open blisters)
- germicidal ointment or wipes
- Vitamin E oil or Bag Balm (optional speed skater remedies)
- ibuprofen
- chemically activated instant ice packs
- copy of medical insurance ID card

Small, commercially prepared first-aid kits are available in better sporting goods stores.

Road Rash Care

Minor road rash can be treated on site and, when cared for properly, will not cause undue scarring or discoloration. But don't be too macho! You should immediately call an ambulance if you cannot stop a wound from bleeding, if it's too severe to clean it yourself, if muscle or bone is visible, or if it is a facial injury that might leave a scar.

Your first priority when treating a new "raspberry" is to clean the wound as soon and as thoroughly as possible. Use soap and water and a clean cloth if available; otherwise scrub it with a sterile gauze pad. This cleaning is likely to hurt, but it's very important because it removes any grit or bacteria that could later cause an infection or scar. Finish off the cleansing by swabbing the raw skin with a germicidal wipe or ointment.

Coat a large but shallow scrape with a membrane-type product after the germicide dries (don't try to apply over ointments). The breathable, flexible membrane promotes healing but prevents the wound from oozing onto your clothes. It sloughs off gradually as the wound heals. Leave smaller wounds (where scabs won't be troublesome) uncovered to air-dry. Speed healing with frequent applications of ointment. Protect tender new skin from the sun to avoid a darkened scar.

For deeper wounds that don't require medical attention, stop the bleeding by raising the limb and applying firm pressure with a sterile gauze pad or cloth. Thoroughly clean the wound; then apply a liberal amount of germicide. Tape a layer of sterile gauze over it to absorb oozing. To promote healing, change the dressing at least twice a day and reapply ointment to prevent a thick, inflexible scab.

Foot Care

Head off blisters and bruises before they occur by getting skates that fit and wearing the right socks. Skate more than an hour and you'll soon regret wearing cotton or trying to make a loose skate fit better with thick socks. They cause slippage, which leads to blisters.

If you have known problem areas, take the preventive approach and apply white athletic tape or Runners Lube (a pain-relieving friction-prevention ointment made by Mueller's Sports Medicine) before you put on your skates. When skating farther than you're used to, pay attention to your feet so you can catch a hot spot before it becomes an out-and-out blister. As soon as you notice such rubbing, stop and cover the area with moleskin. If a blister has already formed, drain it to relieve the pain. Cover an open blister with Second Skin, which acts as a moisture barrier and protects it from friction and pressure. These products are available at your local drugstore.

Soak open blisters once or twice a day in Epsom salts. If you will be skating before a blister is healed, apply one or two peel-and-stick bunion cushions over it, with the holes centered over the blister. This encircles the sore spot with a soft cushion that protects the raw skin from your skate.

Another foot problem that can result from unaccustomed mileage on hard-shell boots is bruising around the ankles. Skate with slightly loosened top buckles to prevent this; once you're bruised it can take up to a week to skate pain-free again.

Handy Accessories

Essential Creature Comforts

Bags, packs, and skate carriers: For day-to-day skating, a small **sports bag** works well for keeping protective gear, accessories, and tools in one place. To carry skates easily, slip a looped **ski boot carrier** under the top buckles. You can also form a makeshift shoulder strap by knotting the skate's

Transpack backpack.

Gene Kliot

laces together or attaching the Velcro ankle straps to each other.

For out-of-town trips, consider the sturdy **travel backpacks** made by Transpack. Skates fit in the side pockets along with socks, a tool kit, and a couple of T-shirts. A helmet, pads, a few more clothes, and toiletries fit in the center compartment, while the pocket on the top flap is big enough for keys, electronics, and suntan lotion.

Having assorted sizes of **fanny packs** makes it easy to choose the smallest useful size for each skate trip. At one extreme, you might use an attractive leather number just large enough for keys, wallet, and cell phone. Larger packs carry those items plus a windbreaker, sandals, and a pair of water bottles stored in external pouches.

Footbeds, insoles, and liners: The more technical your skating, the more important it becomes to translate body finesse through your feet for better pavement precision. Custom footbeds (insoles) are the easiest way to customize skate fit and correct problems with supination (skates tipping onto the inside edges) or pronation (skates tipping onto the outside edges). If you've already got a pair of custom orthotics, try them in your skates. If not, have a pair of cork Superfeet liners heat-molded to your foot shape at your local ski shop, or experiment with drugstore or sporting goods store replacements. To get better cushioning and vibration control, add a cheap pair of Dr. Scholl's liners underneath.

Sunglasses: Good quality sunglasses not only reduce glare so you can see better on bright days, they also cut down on eye fatigue. Eye protection also reduces your chances of getting cataracts as a senior skater. You can also mount a rear-view mirror to a pair of sunglasses.

Water system: How did we ever manage day-long outdoor adventures before personal hydration systems were invented? For people who hate to stop for a drink, a backpack-style water bag with a tube reaching to the lips is just the thing to ward off dehydration on a long skate. These packs usually have a storage pouch or two and a pocket for keys and an energy bar.

Essential Repair Kit Stuff

Skate tools: Keep your tools in a container or pouch small enough to drop into your gear or skate bag. Keep at least two **5/32 Allen wrenches** on hand. These skate keys are standard for most skate bolt systems, and most manufacturers include a wrench with a pair of new skates. Better tools have a **bearing pusher** on one end; this cylindrical nub fits into the same hole the wheel bolts pass through but is wide enough to push the spacer and opposite bearing out the other side of the wheel. It's also a good idea to keep a small **Phillips screwdriver** handy if you need one to replace your brake pad. A **pushpin** is useful for prying out the C-rings that retain the shields on serviceable bearings.

Spare parts: Although collecting extra essential hardware is easier said than done, if you can keep a few spares around, technical difficulties will never prevent you from skating. Keep an extra set of **wheels** on hand, new or used. Collect the right **bolts, spacers,** and **axle guides** for your skates, because there is a wide variation of styles even within a single manufacturer's line. Buy your **heel brakes** three at a time; these also vary by model.

Nice to Have

Apparel: Make use of your T-shirt collection—they're great for skating. For women, jog-bra-style halter tops offer cool support and wicking ability. On chilly days, add a lightweight fleece top or vest. Lycra bike shorts cut down on wind resistance and the noise of flapping cloth. Hide padded shorts with a pair of longer, baggy shorts if you want.

Lights and reflective gear: For skating in low-light situations, buy at least one red flashing light to wear at motorists' eye level and a roll of reflective tape to apply to skates or an old jacket or T-shirt. Some clubs—such as San Francisco's Midnight Rollers—require lights if you're partici-

Skate tools.

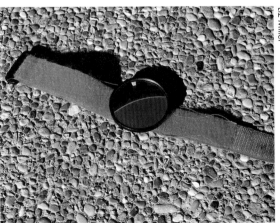

Wrist guard mirror.

Dan Kibler

Liz Miller

pating in a group night skate. A headlamp (available at most mountain outfitters) illuminates the skating surface ahead. You can buy reflective vests, T-shirts, belts, or suspenders from Lentek International (see page 20).

Rear-view mirror: When skating anywhere near automobiles, a wrist guard–mounted rear view mirror makes it easier to keep track of all that's going on around you. If you cannot find a readymade mirror, it's easy to make your own using Velcro, double-sided tape, a web watchband, and a small mirror. Some bicycle stores sell tiny adjustable mirrors for use on sunglasses or helmets.

Great Gadgets

Heart rate monitor: Monitoring and adjusting the intensity of your workouts allows you to optimize your training sessions to gain specific results. Because it's difficult to check your heart rate at a roll, especially when wearing wrist guards, the best tool for the job is a heart rate monitor. The typical unit consists of a chest strap transmitter and a wristwatch-like receiver. Depending on the model, you'll be able to check the time of day, track the duration of your workout, and log how much time you've spent at your targeted training heart rate. During training, the monitor continuously displays your heart rate so you can adjust your intensity according to your goals for that training session. Make sure whatever model you buy can fit around a wrist guard and has control or function buttons that won't accidentally be pushed when you clasp hands behind your back in a tuck. Polar Electro makes several models. See chapter 3 for details on using a heart rate monitor as a training tool.

Nonroll accessories: For those times and places where skating isn't allowed, the Walk and Roll is a small fanny pack that carries a compact pair of slip-on shoes and a few small items. When you aren't skating, it conveniently converts to a hands-free, over-the-shoulder carrying strap. Hyper Walks are small but simple devices made by Hyper Wheels that wedge between two wheels on each skate. A rubber-covered disk at the bottom contacts the ground so you can walk without rolling ("No, really, I'm not skating in here, see?").

Skate computer: Skate computers, such as the one made by Out of Line Sports, report information "at your toetips." Besides distance, a skate computer can track times with a stopwatch, the time of day, miles per hour, and your historical maximum miles per hour. It works with a pair of magnets slipped into opposing sides of the wheel's core; a tiny receiver mounted to the skate frame over that wheel; and a wristwatch-sized computer mounted on the toe of the same skate, wired to the receiver. For best accuracy, you must recalibrate the computer as the wheel becomes worn.

⊙ GEAR RESOURCES

RECOMMENDED SKATE MANUFACTURERS
Bauer USA, Inc., 800-362-3146, <www.bauer.com>
K2 Corporation, 800-426-1617, <www.k2sports.com>
Mission Roller Hockey, 714-556-8856, <www.missionrh.com>
Oxygen, 800-258-5020,

<www.oxygenskates.com> (under construction)
Roces USA, 800-521-2011, <www.roces.it>
Rollerblade, Inc., 800-989-7655, <www.rollerblade.com>
Rossignol, 802-863-2511, <www.rossignolskico.com>
Salomon North America, Inc., 800-225-6850,

<www.salomonsports.com>
Tecnica USA, 800-258-3897, <www.tecnicausa.com>

HELMETS AND PADS
Bauer USA, Inc., 800-362-3146, <www.bauer.com>
Bell Sports, 800-776-5677, <www.bellbikehelmets.com>

(continued on next page)

GEAR RESOURCES *(continued from previous page)*

Giro Sport Design,
800-969-4476,
<www.giro.com>
K2 Corporation, 800-426-1617,
<www.k2sports.com>
Lentek International,
407-857-8786,
<www.lentek.com>
Louis Garneau USA,
802-334-5885,
<www.louisgarneau.com>
Mosa Extreme Sports, Inc.,
310-318-9883,
<www.mosa.com>
(under construction)
Roces USA, 800-521-2011,
<www.roces.it>

Rollerblade, Inc., 800-989-7655,
<www.rollerblade.com>
Triple Eight Products,
800-888-9456,
<www.triple8.com>

OTHER MANUFACTURERS

Hyper Walks, 800-234-9737,
<www.hyperwheels.com>
Lamarjean Group (Skidskins),
888-590-6800,
<www.skidskins.com>
Mueller's Sports Medicine,
800-356-9522, <www.
muellersportsmed.com>
Out of Line Sports,
303-761-4177

Polar Electro Inc.,
800-277-1314,
<www.polarusa.com>
Superfeet Worldwide, LLC,
800-634-6618,
<www.superfeet.com>
Transpack, 212-260-0623,
<www.transpack.net>
Walk and Roll, 888-880-WALK,
<www.walkroll.com>
Wisconsin Pharmacal Co.
(first aid), 414-677-9006,
<www.destinationoutdoors.
com>

CHAPTER TWO

KEY SKILLS FOR THE ADVANCED SKATER

DIALECT

action leg: The leg that performs the work for a given movement (as opposed to the support leg).

aerodynamic tuck: A compact crouch used to reduce wind resistance in which hips, knees, and ankles are flexed deeply, hands are clasped behind the back, and the torso is almost parallel to the ground.

balance: The most important aspect of all advanced skating skills, achieved by constantly adjusting the body position during skating movements to maintain equilibrium. Balance is cumulative over a lifetime and improves along with the skater's fitness level, experience, confidence, and posture.

centerline: An imaginary line that bisects the direction of travel.

center of gravity: The physical point at which body weight is most concentrated, centered along an imaginary line from the belly button to the pubic bone. Muscular contractions and weight shifts (continued on next page)

Although it's exciting to contemplate all the different things you might soon be doing on in-line skates, it's important that you have the requisite abilities to pursue those activities. The remaining chapters in this book list each discipline's prerequisite skills so you know up front whether you're qualified to safely participate or what moves you need to brush up on before proceeding.

What Kind of Skater Are You?

The following lists will help you evaluate your current level of skating. For easy entry to advanced skating, your bag of tricks should already include every skill described here. If it doesn't, any instructor who has been certified at Level 2 by the International Inline Skating Association can teach you the moves. If you're lacking the benefit of a qualified instructor, step-by-step instructions for all listed skills are provided in my first book, *Get Rolling: The Beginner's Guide to In-Line Skating*. Contact the Inline Certification Program listed in the Advanced Skills Resources section at the end of this chapter to find a certified instructor in your area.

Beginner Skills

stride one: The initial "duck walk" stepping stroke used to get first-time skaters rolling gently and slowly forward.

   A-frame turn: A coasting turn made by pressuring the inside wheel edges of one skate while the center of gravity is between both feet.

   Basic stride (a.k.a. stride two): The combination of a short stroke and glide to achieve moderate forward propulsion; typically used by recreational skaters.

DIALECT *(continued from previous page)*

originating in this area affect balance and the base of support for all skating moves.

"nose, knees, toes": Proper body part alignment for an effective power stride when skating in an aerodynamic tuck, a mantra for speed skaters.

push displacement: Stroke length measured from the point of set-down to the fully extended reach of the stroking leg.

ready position: The balanced crouch that results in equilibrium and confidence when learning skating basics. Feet are shoulder width apart and shoulders, hip joints, and arches are balanced in vertical alignment. Knees, hips, and ankles are flexed, and hands and arms are within sight at waist height when coasting.

recovery: The time during which the action leg returns from full extension to set-down.

rotation: Movement in which the head and shoulders twist away from parallel alignment with the pelvis.

stride: The result of combining stroking and gliding.

stroke: The pressuring leg action that propels the skater in forward or backward movement.

support leg: The leg that bears the most weight during movements that require independent legwork.

weight transfer: The shift in the skater's center of gravity over skates and wheel edges.

Dan Kibler

Basic recreational stride.

Heel brake stop: A complete stop made with the skate's standard or cuff-activated brake. (Because so many otherwise competent skaters are unable to use the heel brake for stopping or speed control on hills, a progressive method for learning effective use of the heel brake is included later in this chapter.)

Swizzle: Forward or backward momentum achieved by steering skates in and out in an hourglass pattern, keeping both skates in contact with the ground.

Spin stop: A stop used to terminate forward momentum at low to moderate speeds; initiated with a sharp turn.

Scissors stance: A coasting, turning, and braking stance with skates close together, parallel, and positioned with one skate advanced ahead of the other. The scissors stance is used for coasting over rough surfaces (manhole covers, brick roads, tram tracks, grass), performing advanced turns, and engaging the heel brake.

Parallel turn: A swerving turn executed from a scissors stance with most of the weight on the back skate while the lead skate determines the direction of travel.

Intermediate Skills

Forward crossover: A speed-maintaining turn where the skate on the outside of the corner pushes against its inside wheel edges, and the inside skate crosses under the body while pushing against its outside edges.

Backward skating: Basic backward momentum achieved with a backward version of the swizzle or alternating single-foot swizzles.

Lunge turn: A high-speed version of the parallel turn utilizing a wider scissors stance with the weight distributed equally over both skates.

Forward lunge stop: A stop initiated from a turning lunge over the inside skate while the wheels of the outside skate are sharply angled onto their inside edges and pressed in the direction of travel until the friction terminates movement.

Slalom turn: A series of serpentine turns, usually with the upper body facing downhill, very similar to alpine skiing. See Basic Technique on page 68.

Backward power slide: A backward lunge stop in which the wheels of the stroking skate are swept into the direction of travel while its wheels are sharply angled onto their inside edges and pressed in the direction of travel. See the Forward Power Slide, page 31.

T-stop: A slowing and stopping method executed by placing one skate's wheels across the direction of travel behind the other and dragging to create friction.

Power stride (a.k.a. stride three): Efficient forward propulsion achieved through increased pressure and glide duration, an aerodynamic body position, and a more side-directed leg extension during the push. See Stride Technique.

Directional transitions: The ability to rotate 180 degrees at a roll to transition from forward-to-backward or backward-to-forward skating (including wheel pivots and jumps). See Key Skills on page 116.

Real World Skills

Air: Confident launching off speed bumps, the edges of driveways or wheelchair side cuts on sidewalks, or foot-high skate ramps. See Intro to Street on page 118.

Anticipation: Maintaining constant awareness of the skating surface and environment with the ability to react quickly and safely to sudden changes; the ability to stop or adjust skating speed for a traffic signal or upcoming confluence of trail users.

Speed control: Retaining composure at high speed; the ability to prevent unwanted acceleration on downhills and to stop when and where desired.

Street skills: Gracefully getting up and down curbs, ramps, and stairs; negotiating obstacles (manhole covers, cattle guards, slick or damaged pavement); skating safely near automobiles; making sharp swerves and coasting several yards on one foot.

Uphill skating: A powerful and efficient climbing and sprinting stroke. See Uphill Skating, used for interval training, touring, and skate-to-ski cross training (see page 31).

Even if you don't ever plan to move outside the realm of recreational skating, using the above descriptions as checklists for learning new skills will help you achieve the balance and coordination of the advanced skater.

Stride Technique

Call it a power stride, a speed skater's stride, or "Stride Three." By any name, this caliber of stroking lets you skate faster and harder with less effort. It incorporates an aerodynamic tuck; a front-to-back arm swing (or none at all); a long, lateral push; and, ultimately, set-down on the outside edge to gain the longest possible contact with the pavement during a push.

The power stride is very important to advanced in-line skating, no matter what activities you pursue. To learn it without developing bad habits, spend a few weeks working on your aerodynamic tuck, skating without the use of your arms and focusing on long, side-directed pushes as described below. After you've developed enough balance and strength to feel comfortable skating this way, begin to incorporate use of the outside edge. See page 26 in this chapter.

Aerodynamic Tuck

Bending your torso even slightly to decrease wind resistance conserves precious energy for a long skate. It might take a few months of practice before you can maintain a tuck for more than a few minutes without experiencing a backache.

To get into position the first time, fold your hands together and place your knuckles under your chin; then touch your elbows to your knees. This results in the desired torso position ("nose, knees, toes") and proper flex at the hips, knees, and ankles. Now, place both hands behind your back and clasp hands. For the most aerodynamic and energy-efficient tuck, follow this preflight checklist, both standing still and while skating:

____ Skates parallel and shoulder width apart, with wheels perpendicular to the pavement.

____ Body weight positioned slightly behind midfoot to maximize forceful, full-skate push-offs.

____ Knees flexed at 110–120 degrees (the thighs are almost parallel to the pavement); flexing at the ankles makes it much easier to position the knees over the toes.

____ Upper body angled forward at 45 degrees; the spine can be rounded slightly, shoulders point forward, and head and eyes stay up. *Tip: Be careful you don't tip your center of gravity ahead of your feet, or you'll diminish your ability to make a strong push from the heels.*

____ Arms folded close to the body, with hands clasped at the small of the back.

____ In movement, the nose is always over the gliding knee, which is over the same leg's toes ("nose, knees, toes").

 PRACTICE TIP

On a long straightaway, practice holding a tuck for as long as you can. If your lower back starts aching, try shifting your weight closer to your back wheels or letting your shoulders and elbows droop slightly toward the ground. Tip your pelvis forward to relax the tension in your lower back without changing your upper body angle.

Arm Swing

A forceful, side-to-side swing is useful for short sprints on a game court, race starts and breakaways, and getting up hills. Otherwise, the sideways swing is the telltale mark of an inefficient skater. Straight-legged beginners resort to literally

Finding your aerodynamic tuck.

throwing their weight away from the inside edge rather than pushing from a well-flexed leg.

Once you learn to stay in balance as you shift your weight from one extending leg to the other, a full arm swing is no longer necessary. A front-to-back swing contributes to forward propulsion when you want to pick up speed. But you'll find a two-handed swing becomes more hindrance than help over a long haul, when energy conservation is important. If you don't have good enough balance to skate with both hands behind your back, take just one arm out of play at first.

PRACTICE TIP

Use the proper arm swing while skating in an aerodynamic tuck. With palms facing in, swing one hand forward as the other swings back. The back-swinging arm passes close to the hip and ends with the little finger pointing skyward. That arm is straight. The front-swinging hand ends with the thumb between the nose and opposite shoulder. The right leg completes a stroke with full leg extension at the same time the left thumb reaches the nose, and vice versa.

Stride Angle and Duration

Keep the stroking skate parallel to the direction of travel during each stroke, even as you push it directly to the side. To further increase the length of each stroke, recover your pushing skate fully back under your hips before you set it back down.

Try this stationary demonstration. Standing in an aerodynamic tuck with your skates across a line, shift your weight to one foot and extend the opposite skate directly to the side as far up the line as possible. This distance represents your maximum stroke length. See what happens when you extend your skate more to the back or straighten your knees. These are the technique glitches that can shorten your push and reduce efficiency.

PRACTICE TIP

While skating in a tuck

- Attempt to push the right skate's heel wheel toward a two o'clock position with each stroke and the left toward ten o'clock.
- Be sure to keep all wheels in contact with the pavement throughout the entire length of every stroke.
- Concentrate on pushing with the heel wheel to prevent inefficient "toe flicking."
- Once the entire skate leaves the pavement, steer that toe along an imaginary semicircle behind you until it passes ahead of the support skate. Imagine it is tracing a letter D over the pavement.
- To ensure full recovery, do not return the pushing skate to the pavement until you are aligned "nose, knees, toes."

You'll find that this type of skating results in a slower stroke tempo.

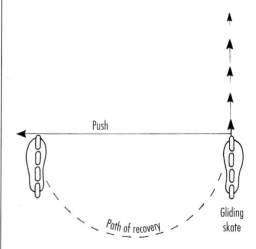

The toe traces a D on recovery.

Balance and Strength

Take a few weeks to get used to the speed, pushing force, and demands for balance that result from longer strokes and glides and skating with your arms behind your back. If necessary, spend extra time doing one-footed balance drills or tricks to make that long glide seem easier. Plan on a few months for your back to adjust to extended periods in a tuck. Because good stroke technique requires rock-solid hip stability, regular sessions of lower back, hip, hamstring, and quadriceps resistance training will speed up this phase of learning.

If you've recently made the transition to five-wheel skates, get to know them by tinkering with the fit and lacing strategies and get used to maneuvering with the longer frame. If they're brakeless, learn how to slow down and stop both on the flats and slopes. See Hill Skills on page 28.

The following drills teach you how to gain the further advantage of outside edge stroke initiation. After you've mastered them, resume work on your tuck, stride angle, and duration, this time employing a set-down on the outside edge.

Utilizing the Outside Edge

You can add another inch or two to your already extended stroke length by optimizing skate recovery. Do this by returning the skate to the pavement beyond the invisible centerline. Due to the lateral weight shift toward the recovering leg that results from a push, you can set the recovered skate back down on its outside wheel edges. During the glide, the weight shifts back toward the new recovering leg, which tips the gliding skate from its outside edge, across the wheel apex, and onto its inside edge into the next pushing stroke. This moment is where the most powerful surge of force occurs.

OUTSIDE EDGE SWIZZLES

Use the following swizzle/scooter progression to get comfortable with initiating a push from your outside edge.

1. Assume a tuck and begin a series of forward swizzles, steering both skates out and in, tracing an hourglass pattern.

2. At the moment when your feet are closest together, allow both ankles to relax outward so that your skates tip onto their outside wheel edges.

3. As the skates separate to begin a new push, they will naturally roll onto the inside edges. Finish the outward push by pressuring the heel wheels and steering the toes inward.

4. After you get the feel of a bilateral push, align your weight over the left skate and do a series of scooters, pushing the right skate directly to the side by rolling it from the outside to inside edges.

5. Switch legs to perform scooters on the opposite side.

STRADDLE THE CENTERLINE

Practice setting the recovered skate down beyond the centerline to gain added stroke length. Try this crossed-skates drill standing still before attempting it at a roll.

1. Coasting in a moderate speed tuck, lift one skate, pass it in front of and across the other, and return it to the ground about two or three inches beyond the other skate.

2. Equalize your weight over both sets of outside edges, making note of the pressure under the outer portion of both feet. Keep the skates parallel.

3. Get used to rolling in this position with either foot crossed in front.

THREE-EDGE STROKES

Get more familiar with your edges by skating down a straight visible line.

1. Moving at a moderate speed in a tuck, begin a series of scooters (see page 42).

2. At first, return the action skate to the pavement directly in front of the support skate, right on top of the centerline.

ROLL MODEL

One fine day I met Matt, who possessed an impressive glossary of skate terms, including *bashing*.

"What's that?" I asked.

"Skating down stairs."

"Show me."

He rolled me straight to the "course"—three steps.

The steps actually grew longer the closer I got. I hit them not with grace or style but with a splat. I got up, wiped off my purple shorts, and made several more attempts, wobbling like a three-wheeled wagon filled with 6-year-olds. Strangers paused to watch my bravery.

"Just relax!" Matt shouted. The last time someone said that to me I was 40 and in labor. Then, too, I faced fear, pain, and a desire to do away with witnesses. With a final breath I successfully "bashed" those cement monsters. After facing that taunting tarmac, I felt ready to take on the rest of the planet—on *my* terms.

I was not an accomplished athlete prior to skating, and I don't live in that type of a body, though I grew up believing life would begin as soon as I did. In-line skating empowers me to do what those sleek Spandex bearers do and accept myself, "power thighs" and all. Now I thrive on experiences and events that I used to think only "other people" could do. This thinking, which used to stop me before I got started, has taken me far.

—Suzan Davis, freelance writer; skate instructor; fitness promoter; and founder of Babes on Blades, formerly a Sacramento-area skating club—now a frame of mind

3. Next, try to land the action skate beyond the centerline before pushing it into a stroke. Keep the wheels parallel to the centerline throughout the stroke.

4. Begin setting the action skate down on its outside edge, still beyond the centerline. Continue until you experience a small surge of power as the stroke evolves from an outside edge to an inside edge push.

5. Repeat with your other foot.

HALF POWER STRIDES

Begin incorporating outside edge landings into your stroke by working on just one foot at a time. Once you've mastered doing this with each leg independently, put it all together and practice at every opportunity.

1. In your best form, build up to your highest comfortable speed and get into a

Stroking from the outside edge.

Dan Kibler

steady stroking rhythm. Remember to extend sideways, not back.

2. Begin concentrating on setting down your favorite skate on its outside edge beyond the directional centerline. Try to ignore your other skate.

3. Seek a feeling of pressure along the outside edge of your action skate each time it hits the pavement; feel the short pull as it rolls from its outside to its inside wheel edges and begins a push.

4. Once you can consistently achieve this kinetic feedback on one side, start practicing on the opposite leg's push and setdown.

5. Finally, build up to a full power stride by initiating both right and left strokes from an outside edge landed beyond the centerline.

Hill Skills

When scouting for hills to practice on, look for varying inclines of debris- and traffic-free pavement in good repair with a long (better yet, uphill) runout. In a real-world situation, you might combine two or three of these control techniques on a given hill. Learn to adapt your style to the pitch of the hill and your current abilities.

Heel Brake Stop

Excellent heel brake technique is essential for dealing with hills, intersections, traffic, and unpredictable trail users. Hockey and aggressive skaters manage to survive with T-stops, lunge stops, and power slides because in most cases they stick to fairly flat terrain. Speed skaters sacrifice the few ounces a brake weighs for the sake of speed and rely on T-stops, slalom turns, and agility to avoid danger on racecourses.

Many intermediate to advanced skaters have never learned how to use a heel brake properly, because unfortunately (and this is the bane of in-line skating) the heel brake is not as easy to use as it looks! Simply raising the toe of the braking skate while the pad is directly below the hips is actually dangerous, because the body tends to keep moving when the feet stop. Here's what you need to know.

● The brake pad must be directly in your line of travel; otherwise, every attempt to use it will end in a turn. The best way to move the brake front and center is to start from a coasting scissors stance with most of your weight shifted back over a well-bent support leg.

● To gain more leverage, lower your center of gravity behind the brake. The most common mistake is leaning the upper body forward ahead of the brake, which actually reduces friction. The more you lower your center of gravity *behind* the brake, the more your own weight can compound the friction on the pad. The best way to lower your center of gravity is to bend your support leg knee while keeping your torso upright.

● Maintain a narrow stance and keep both skates pointing in the same direction until you complete the stop.

The heel brake stop evolves from a coasting ready position to a crouched scissors stance to a light brake drag to deftly dropping the hips at the desired stopping point. Performing these moves in smooth sequence results in stopping success. Conversely, rushing through or skipping any of these maneuvers will hinder your efforts at stopping and speed control. If you need more than the information presented above, review the moves one at a time by performing the following progression of stopping drills.

SCISSORS STANCE

Besides serving as an approach for heel brake stops, a scissors stance is the best position for gliding safely and easily over nasty patches of pavement, because the wheels form a longer platform that provides better front-to-back stability.

1. At a moderate speed, begin coasting in proper ready position, with knees, hips, and ankles well bent, feet shoulder width apart, and hands in view.

2. Shift most of your weight over the support (nonbraking) leg. The required narrow stance occurs more naturally when you do this.

3. With knee pads touching, push the brake skate ahead of the same leg's knee. Bend the support leg so you can advance the heel brake well ahead of the other skate's toe. From a side view, your lower legs should form a triangle over the pavement surface, with knees forming the top point.

4. Make sure your skates are parallel, they are no more than three inches apart, and both toes are pointing forward.

Cuff-activated brake users: Pushing the toe ahead of the knee to assume a scissors stance causes the calf muscle to move the cuff of the skate backward, which moves the brake arm down, which engages the brake. To roll in the scissors stance without braking, keep the forward skate's knee directly over the toe instead of behind it and stagger the knees wider front-to-back rather than just the skates.

BALANCED DRAGGING

This component of braking also serves as the all-important "cruise control" that prevents unwanted acceleration on a long downhill.

1. Stride to gain a moderate speed; then relax into a coasting ready position with hands waist high and in view.

2. Assume the scissors stance with 80 percent of your body weight shifted onto the support leg (the nonbraking leg). Keep your torso upright with your chest pointing ahead, not down.

3. Engage the brake and lightly drag it on the pavement. Try to hear, feel, and pro-

long the light contact but don't try to stop yet. Remember to keep the brake ahead of your body mass—which means don't lean forward!

- **Standard brakes:** Lift the toe of the brake skate until the rubber touches the pavement enough to drag lightly.

- **Cuff-activated brakes:** Press the big toe in the braking skate downward onto the pavement as you scissors that boot ahead of the knee. If the brake doesn't touch the ground, lower the brake pad and/or bend the support leg's knee further.

4. Practice until your balance is good enough to maintain a light drag for several yards in a straight line. Keep your upper body upright, with shoulders over hips and hips over heels.

DISTANCE PLANNING

1. Repeat the above drill, but this time try to stop by gradually squeezing on more brake pad pressure. Do this by sinking lower over the support leg and pushing the pad farther ahead (not down).

PRACTICE TIP

If the narrow stance feels difficult at first, tuck the support knee behind the braking knee or perform braking with both knees touching throughout the move.

2. Quickly straighten up or resume skating after each fast stop to avoid loss of balance.

- **To stop whenever and wherever you need to,** practice assertive stops on a real or imaginary line at different approach speeds. Start with an upright torso so that when the force of the stop pulls your shoulders forward, they have someplace to go. Resist that pull by tightening up your abdominal muscles.

- **To make using the heel brake instinctive,** make many practice stops, learning how much distance you need to stop at a specific spot for any given speed or downhill pitch. Engage the brake lightly as you roll down long, gentle slopes to learn speed control on hills. Finally, practice making complete stops midhill.

- **To make it "smoke,"** you should be able to briefly balance *all* your weight on the brake pad after completing an assertive stop (in other words, lifting the back skate totally off the pavement).

Used correctly, a heel brake makes the shortest, easiest stops.

Dan Kibler

Speed Control

When the slope ahead is a long one, it's important to start controlling your speed early, even if the grade doesn't look visibly steep. Skates with good wheels and bearings can very quickly accelerate to uncomfortable speeds. Your perception of the pitch as "steep" or "gentle" will evolve as your skills do, so it's best to learn brakeless tactics in the following sequence.

HEEL BRAKE

Coasting in a scissors position with the brake lightly engaged is the easiest way to prevent unwanted speed buildup, no matter how long the hill.

SNOWPLOW

The snowplow ("slowplow" if you must) is a ski technique that you can use both for speed control and stopping. Swizzle both skates out to the side with equal pressure. The wider you can get them from the start and the stronger your outer hip muscles, the more you slow down. Keep your torso upright and your hips low as you push against your edges so that your body mass stays behind both skates to compound the pressure. It's easier to stay low and wide if you concentrate on keeping the skates upright and off the inside wheel edges.

TRAVERSE

If there's enough room and nobody is close on your heels, traverse the slope by skating across the fall line (the imaginary line from the top of the hill to the bottom), spending as little time as possible with your wheels pointed directly downhill. Make sequential turns—preferably parallel turns, because all eight wheels are on edge, creating friction. To stop downhill progress, prolong a turn until you are skating back uphill.

SLALOM

Moderate pitches are perfect for a long series of slalom turns. Depending on your edging technique, you can either enjoy a giant slalom ski-style run with very little speed control or dig in with tighter, more edge-pressured turns across the fall line. See Slowing Slaloms, page 129.

T-STOP

Slip into a T-stop position with enough pressure to prevent unwanted acceleration but not so much that balance is compromised. Quickly switch feet if you get tired; for safety's sake, learn to drag either skate with equal balance and effectiveness.

WALK

When sizing up a hill, be sure you factor in the impact of environmental conditions that contribute indirectly to its steepness: overall length, bad light, surface conditions, and traffic, to name a few. If things look too dicey, dare to be a wimp. Some hills are just too dangerous for skating, no matter how good you are. Recognize the maximum gradient you can handle and be mature enough to hike down rather than risk injury.

Bailing Out

When you're skating brakeless, there may be times when your attempts at speed control have failed and you realize you've got to "bail" off a slope. Take immediate action: Don't ever assume you can just ride out a hill lacking a safe runout. This type of thinking will have you cruising for a bruising while your speed picks up even more, and there are too many sad stories about skaters who unsuccessfully fell prey to it. I still have a scar from my own hopeful schuss during my innocent early days.

The moment you recognize a bail situation, immediately get into a crouched scissors stance with your hands forward and your weight evenly distributed on both skates. Then choose the safest spot to make one of the following (progressively dire) maneuvers.

- Gain the unpaved roadside by rolling or running to a stop, making a baseball-style dive, or sliding on your bottom. Be prepared to hop a curb on the way.

- Drop forward into a controlled slide on your pads.

- Tuck into a shoulder roll, directing it in the direction that seems safest.

Uphill Skating

Because your glide is much shorter going up a steep hill, climbing requires a strong, quick stroke, a good body position, and a well-directed arm swing, all in one fluid movement. If it's a long hill, be sure to pace yourself, because steep climbs can literally take your breath away.

Body position: To gain the most power on each stroke, crouch slightly uphill by curving your shoulders forward. The weight of your torso and hips must be directly over your flexed heels in order to deliver the most powerful push. Besides allowing you to push with the proper muscles, a proper crouch also reduces the likelihood of a backache later on. As you climb, keep your shoulders facing uphill.

Stroke: Position the stroking skate 45 degrees to the incline to ensure a good grip. (Skiers will recognize this as the same herringbone position used to skate the flats or hike uphill on skis.) At the end of each short stroke, drive the recovering knee as far uphill as possible before returning the skate to the pavement. On very steep climbs, skating this way almost looks like you are running up the hill, especially when performed at high speed.

Arms: Keep your hands pointed up the hill and elbows slightly bent. Instead of the front-to-back movement you use on the flats, use a sprinting swing, which is more side directed. Each time you push off, punch both arms forcefully away from the stroking skate. This uses your body weight to throw pressure onto the wheel edges, which helps maintain momentum between each stroke.

Forward Power Slide

All forms of the power slide are used for stops and sudden direction changes during in-line hockey play, where heel brakes are rarely used. The "slide" part is done on the inside sidewalls of the extended skate's wheels. This both looks and feels really cool.

Warning: This move is too complicated to be safe as a stopping method on hills.

Slick concrete such as a painted basketball or volleyball court is best for learning power slides; a smooth surface makes it easier (and safer) to slip along with the least possibility of pavement irregularities to catch your wheels. Shorten your learning curve by using a line or object on the pavement as a spotting aid.

There are four possible front power slide combinations, depending on which direction you like to spin and which leg you use for braking. The following drills help you learn a power slide that starts from a counterclockwise spin and ends with the right skate extended, the easiest of the four versions to learn (for right-handers). It consists of a setup **parallel turn** toward the right, a pivoting **spin** toward the left, and a finishing **backward power slide**.

For your learning ease, each component is described separately in the following step-by-step drills. Stay loose and low and get good at a move before moving on to the next power slide component. We'll pull them all together in a final drill.

Be prepared to practice a lot; this is one skill that is rarely learned in a day. But don't overdo it. The extreme lunge position puts you at greater risk for falls or a pulled groin muscle, and if you practice too enthusiastically, the repetitive twisting can give you a sore back. Pay close attention to wheel wear, too. Power slides tend to result in flat spots. If your wheel bolts drag across the pavement, they risk damage too. Still interested? Thought so!

Parallel Turn

If necessary, warm up first with parallel turns toward the left. That's the easiest direction for right-handed skaters. However, when used as a precursor for the power slide described below (also preferred by right-handers), the setup swerve is toward the right, as is the following drill. The right skate advances to make a right parallel turn; the left skate advances to make a left turn.

1. Skating forward, scissors the right skate one length ahead, keeping a very narrow stance so both sets of wheels are almost tracing a single arc.

2. Shift most of your weight onto the trailing left skate while twisting your upper body and hips toward the right.

3. Lean toward the center of the turn with your weight distributed 75 percent on the left skate and 25 percent on the back two wheels of the right skate. Keep all wheels on the pavement.

4. Both skates will curve to the right, tilted onto their right edges. Commit to the tilt by twisting your hips and left knee to the right, toward the center of the turn.

Spin Stop

A forward power slide incorporates the first half of a spin stop. For easier spins, commit to the rotation by swinging outstretched arms toward the left during the move.

1. Coasting forward, look over your left shoulder and start an A-frame (wide-stance) turn to the left.

2. In that half-second when your weight has transferred to your right skate, lift the left skate's heel and pivot it quickly into a heel-to-heel position.

3. Return the left heel to the pavement and equalize your balance on both feet to complete the spin, knees out and heels in.

Backward Power Slide

For best results, look over your right shoulder at a mark or object in the direction of travel and fix your gaze there until you come to a stop. The support leg skate simply rolls backward throughout the movement.

1. Skating backward in a coasting roll, sink into a crouch with your eyes fixed on

your mark behind you. Look over the right shoulder.

2. Maintaining a lunge over your left knee, push the right skate to the side and begin to sweep it into the direction of travel. As the right skate extends behind the body, it tips steeply onto its sidewalls and begins to slide.

3. Once the right skate's wheels are perpendicular to the direction of travel, rise slightly from your lunge to better leverage the pressure on the pavement.

Putting It All Together

1. Skating forward, approach your stopping mark at a moderate speed. Twenty feet out, raise both arms to the sides, propeller-style.

2. Scissors the right skate ahead and swing your left hand in front and your right hand in back as you make an abbreviated right parallel turn with most of your weight on the left skate. This is the clockwise "windup" for the spin.

3. With your eyes fixed in the direction of travel, transfer most of your weight *briefly* to the right skate while steering it left. The moment the left skate is unweighted, pivot it 180 degrees on the toe wheel. At the same time, assertively swing your outstretched arms counterclockwise 180 degrees.

4. Sink into a deep crouch over your left knee and finish sweeping your right skate into the direction of travel. As your right inside sidewalls cross the line of travel, momentum and your lunge over the backward left skate will allow it to slide.

5. To finish the stop, rise slightly from the lunge to increase the right skate's pressure on the pavement.

PRACTICE TIP

If your right skate's wheels skip across the pavement instead of sliding, start from a lower lunge over the left knee (or find smoother pavement).

Finishing a power slide.

Dan Kibler

Coordination

The most noticeable trait of the advanced skater is a confident, balanced style. This is not a result of hours or years spent simply skating forward. Skating agility comes from a willingness to experiment with new positions and moves. This type of play improves balance and coordination across the spectrum of skating skills and beyond, to other athletic pursuits. It's true that many of the drills below could be interpreted as stunts to impress your friends, but by learning these moves you will dramatically increase your advanced skating credentials.

Heel-Toe Roll

The following instructions assume the brake is on the right skate (otherwise it will catch and trip you!).

1. Coasting at a moderate pace with your feet shoulder width apart, pick up your right heel and allow your right toe wheel to bear about half of your body weight. Let the right wheel trail 3 to 6 inches behind the left skate.

2. In one quick movement, push your left skate ahead (it might help to throw your hands up to the sides to briefly lighten the load on your feet). As the left knee straightens, the left toe lifts off the pavement. Now you are rolling on just one heel wheel and one toe wheel.

3. Once you can roll on one toe and one heel wheel, see how far you can spread your skates and how low you can get to the ground.

Double Toe Roll

Once you've got the heel-toe roll, you're ready to try rolling on both toe wheels at the same time. This is possible both forward and backward.

1. Begin coasting at a moderate pace with your feet shoulder width apart.

2. Pick up your right heel and allow your right toe wheel to bear about half of your body weight as it rolls 3 to 6 inches behind your left heel.

3. Now lift the left skate's heel off the pavement. Well-flexed knees allow the heels to lift higher.

Turn on a Line

Use painted parking space lines to trigger a series of 180- or 360-degree transitions: either pivoting or hops (see Directional Transitions, page 116). Fix your eyes on a line before and during each transition as a helpful spotting aid. Practice combinations in both clockwise and counterclockwise directions and mix it up until you can't surprise yourself. This drill is worth much repetition, because it results in smooth and confident transitions at varying speeds in any direction.

Teaching Others

Becoming a Certified Instructor

If you get along well with all types of people and enjoy showing others what you've learned on skates, you are an ideal candidate to become a certified in-line skating instructor. The International Inline Skating Association's Inline Certification Program teaches a standard instruction methodology that is used worldwide.

ICP Level 1 is a certification for teaching beginner skills, while Level 2 certifies the teaching of intermediates. Instructor candidates must successfully complete a training course and testing that involves a written exam, a practical teaching exam, and a skating skills test. At Level 2, in addition to learning how to teach a selection of intermediate skills, the candidate's overall professionalism, ability to offer troubleshooting tips, and industry knowledge are added to the test. The Master Level, open to both Level 1 and Level 2 instructors, certifies candidates for a specific skating discipline such as fitness or speed skating.

Certification programs are held over a three-day weekend in major metropolitan areas across the country and internationally. Advance registration is required. The certified instructor's annual liability insurance and ICP membership dues are $125. A weekend certification clinic costs about $325, which includes these fees. Certified instructors participate in various activities each year (including teaching) to earn continuing education points for later renewal.

As for your own abilities, for the initial Level 1 certification you must be proficient at and able to teach basic stroking and gliding, swizzles, simple turns, stopping with a heel brake, and the T-stop, among other moves. You'll also have to demonstrate proficiency in backward skating, parallel and lunge turns, slaloms, and crossovers. Although you won't be trained to teach these, they are skills that are covered in the Level 2 certification, and Level 1 candidates are required to be capable of performing all Level 2 skills to prove their competency as skaters.

Teaching others to skate.

In addition to certification, the IISA also sponsors regional chapters of the National Skate Patrol, a community-based program that certifies groups of skaters to provide basic instruction, safety tips, and first aid wherever large groups of skaters gather. To join your local chapter or set the wheels in motion to organize a new chapter, contact the IISA's NSP division (see the appendix).

For more information about what's expected of instructor candidates and the dates and locations of each year's certification sites, call 216-371-2977 or visit the ICP webpage at <*www.iisa.org/icp*>.

Instructing Your Child

Skating can be a healthy pastime even for families with smaller children who haven't yet developed the balance and coordination required to learn in-line skills. The littlest ones can be pushed in a jogging stroller while big brother or sister rides along on a tricycle or bike (with training wheels, if necessary). The parent pushing the stroller must be a competent skater, capable of using the heel brake to stop and control speed. It's a good idea to first practice maneuvering a stroller without the child in it to gain some experience lifting the front wheel(s) to get over curbs and make tight turns.

Most youngsters develop the necessary motor skills to learn skating at about 6 or 7 years old. Before that age, a pair of toy skates might help them get used to rolling. In a few rare cases, however, children as young as 3 or 4 have demonstrated incredible early aptitude on regular in-line skates.

If youth lessons from a certified instructor aren't available, a patient parent can begin teaching a child the in-line basics as long as he or she uses a positive and encouraging tone throughout the lesson. Any sign of impatience or frustration on your part is instantly obvious to your child and might result in a power struggle that could plague every future teaching effort. Quit as soon as fatigue or wandering attention (yours or your child's) starts making the lesson less fun. That way, there

Kids love learning to skate.

will always be another day to pick up where you left off.

Use games and imagery your child can relate to.

- Make falling seem fun by encouraging the child to land loudly on protective gear.

- Refer to "Frankenstein" or "robot" turns when teaching the A-frame turn.

- Skate "like a flamingo" to teach one-footed balance and weight shift.

- Talk about the game of tug-of-war when describing proper heel brake position and play red light–green light to practice stops.

- Play Simon Says to practice a variety of skills while skating in a big circle.

- Use chalk to draw on the pavement: a line for practicing stopping, a lemon shape for learning swizzles, or a curvy train track to enforce a wide stance for A-frame turns.

- Set obstacle courses with cones or have the child pick up objects from the pavement for general motor skills improvement.

Stick to a smooth, traffic-free location until your child can confidently demonstrate striding, turning, and effective use of the heel brake for slowing and stopping. Next, familiarize your child with the Rules of the Road (see page 59) to make sure he or she understands the etiquette and safety guidelines expected of all trail skaters, especially the importance of staying to the right side of the trail. Only then should you try an outing on a public path.

ADVANCED SKILLS RESOURCES

ORGANIZATIONS

Inline Certification Program (ICP)
Kris Simeone, Director
P.O. Box 18309
Cleveland Heights OH 44118
216-371-2977
fax 216-371-6270
E-mail: Icpinline@aol.com
www.iisa.org/icp

VIDEOS

Skate Great. Eden Prairie MN:

Rollerblade, Inc., 1997,
800-232-7665,
<www.rollerblade.com>.

PUBLICATIONS

Get Rolling: The Beginner's Guide
to In-Line Skating. Liz Miller.
Camden ME: Ragged Mountain Press, 1998.
Inline! A Manual of Intermediate
to Advanced Technique.
William Nealy. Birmingham AL:

Menasha Ridge Press, 1998.
In-Line Skater Magazine
4099 McEwen Dr., Suite 350
Dallas TX 75244-5039
214-742-2000
E-mail: skater@flc.mhs.
compuserve.com
In-Line Skating: A Complete Guide
for Beginners (children's book
for ages 8 to 14). George Sullivan. New York: Puffin Books,
1993.

Dan Kibler

Dan Kibler

CHAPTER THREE

FITNESS SKATING

DIALECT

aerobic fitness: A level of cardiorespiratory efficiency determined by the heart's ability to pump oxygenated blood from the lungs to the working muscles and then return unused deoxygenated blood back to the lungs for reoxygenation. Aerobic fitness is determined by measuring maximum oxygen consumption (VO_2 max).

aerobic interval training: Exercise performed at 80 to 85 percent of maximum heart rate for 3–5 minutes, followed by 3–5 minutes of recovery. This is an excellent entry level for those new to interval training.

anaerobic interval training: Exercise performed at 85 to 95 percent of maximum heart rate for 30–90 seconds to the point of breathlessness, followed by a recovery period that is two to three times as long as the interval.

anaerobic threshold (AT): The heart rate at which the body's (continued on next page)

One memorable day, as you scoot past yet another bicyclist on the trail, you realize you can skate much farther than you used to, and in less time. You don't feel tired until you've covered several miles, and you love it. You wonder, "What would happen if I put some effort into this? What could I accomplish if I set some fitness goals and applied myself?"

Hold that thought. Before beginning any new exercise program, it's wise to get a physical examination by your doctor. Besides ensuring you're fit enough for the new workload and uncovering any problems up front, an exam is a good opportunity to record your baseline "before" state, so you can better measure your improvements. As you continue your fitness lifestyle, you should see a lower resting heart rate and blood pressure and improved cholesterol and blood fat levels.

Liz Miller

A purposeful workout.

DIALECT (continued from previous page)

capacity to flush away the buildup of lactic acid from the muscles is exceeded by its rate of lactic acid production. Also known as *lactic threshold* or *LT*.

balance: The body's automatic response to maintain equilibrium.

elite athlete: A competitor who has achieved a peak athletic performance level, usually through periodization training.

fitness skater: A skater who uses in-line workouts to maintain or improve fitness or to prepare for fitness division participation in speed skating races.

flexibility: The degree of range of motion in the body's joints.

half swizzle: Executing swizzles by gliding on one skate while repeatedly swizzling the other skate out and in with its wheels in constant contact with the ground.

heart rate: The frequency of heart muscle contractions spanning the range from its lowest resting rate to a maximum rate that decreases with age; useful for measuring intensity of workload.

maximum heart rate (MHR): An individual's calculated or tested upper limit of heart muscle contractions per minute.

muscular endurance: The amount of time a muscle or group of muscles can continue the same movement

without performance degradation due to fatigue; for example, the ability to maintain good stroke technique when tired.

muscular strength: From a skating perspective, the amount of force generated during each stroke's contraction and extension.

periodization: A strategy of varying workout focus and gradually increasing volume and intensity over distinct time periods (cycles) to prevent stagnation and maximize the desired physiological adaptations.

plyometric training: An advanced form of jump training designed to link strength with speed of movement to produce power.

In-Line Workout Benefits

Fun as it is, skating contributes directly to the most sought-after exercise goals: improved aerobic fitness, strength, endurance, and body fat reduction. Fast-paced skating has been proven to be just as aerobically beneficial as running; compared to cycling, an equal skating effort results in a better muscular workout for hips, thighs, and shins. As long as you apply yourself to purposeful workouts with specific daily goals (as opposed to simply going through the motions), you are setting yourself up to enjoy the maximum possible benefits from fitness skating.

Better aerobic fitness: The benefits of sustained aerobic exercise have been acknowledged for years. On skates, 25 minutes—universally acknowledged as the minimum for improving aerobic capacity—seems much too soon to stop, especially after the natural high from the release of endorphins kicks in! Unlike running or some health club aerobics options, skating doesn't in-volve the jarring footfall that is so hard on overused or aging lower body joints. To ice the cake, because it's a weight-bearing activity, an in-line workout also contributes to bone density as your aerobic fitness improves.

Strength gains: Consistent skate training has been found to tone and build stronger and more stable pelvis, hip, and leg muscles. The quadriceps—the muscles on the fronts of the thighs—are strengthened both from the sustained isometric contraction while gliding in a tuck position and from the repeated contractions and extensions of stroking. Each stroke puts hamstrings, buttocks, and hip flexors into play for balance and propulsion, while the abdominals and lower back remain contracted to stabilize the upper body. This also works the adductors (inner thigh, pulling muscle) and the abductors (outer thigh, pushing muscle). If you're new to such athletic workouts, you'll notice these muscles feeling gradually firmer and more toned.

The low weight–high repetitions of the in-line skating stride's push-off strengthen spinal erectors (lower back muscles). For people with unstable disks in the lower back, a few weeks of skating workouts is an excellent way to make this area stronger and less achy. People recovering from knee surgery have found that skating is a quick way to rehabilitate the muscles in that complex joint.

Improved endurance: An in-line skating training program can increase muscular as well as aerobic endurance. Adopt a weekly in-line interval training session such as repeated uphill sprints, and your skating muscles—in conjunction with the cardiovascular system—begin to utilize the body's energy stores more efficiently, increasing your capacity for prolonged hard work. Long, slow distance skating improves aerobic fitness, which in turn allows you to skate even longer without fatigue.

Body fat reduction: A consistent 25 minutes of aerobic activity three to five times a week can gradually turn your body into a fat-burning machine. As your muscles get firmer and denser, your body burns more calories, even when you're asleep! As long as you keep the pace above 10 miles per hour, in-line skating burns the same number of calories as running.

Gear

Fitness improvements come sooner for those who are properly outfitted. Details about the items in **bold type** below are found in chapter 1, Equipping Your Sports Closet.

Skates

The more time you spend on skates, the more important it is to have a comfortable fit. Your attempts at in-line workouts will suffer unless your feet are pain free and your body movements are efficiently translated to your skates. Fitness skates are designed to meet these needs. Learn about the features to look for below and then review Shopping for Skates on page 9.

A fitness **boot** maximizes comfort and usually is composed of nonplastic materials similar to a sport shoe, although many feature a plastic cuff or buckle. A soft boot constructed of lightweight,

Salomon North America

Fitness skates by Salomon.

breathable material keeps feet relatively cool. In some cases, the boot material can be heat molded to fit your foot. Fitness skates usually have a lower cuff to allow more ankle flexibility, which in turn allows longer strokes and a less tiring tuck position but requires stronger ankle muscles. If you own a pair of prescription orthotics or other **custom footbeds** that fit in your skates, use them to fill any gaps that might prevent your foot movements from translating directly to your equipment.

The wheel **frame** on a fitness skate is longer than a recreational skate's to provide more stability at high speeds. Some models accommodate five wheels to increase push traction, although an extended wheel base makes skates less maneuverable and using a heel brake more awkward.

Taller **wheels** (76 to 80 mm) with a narrow profile reduce friction from road contact. Although wheels with those few extra millimeters raise your center of gravity, they can also smooth out the ride. Good quality **bearings** (ABEC 3 or higher) decrease rolling resistance. Because most outdoor skating routes are fairly gritty, don't spend money on higher-rated bearings unless you're entering a race. For outdoor fitness skating, use 76A–80A durometer (hardness) for better grip and less vibration on asphalt and roads.

Attire, Protection, and Accessories

When preparing for a long workout on skates, wear close-fitting **athletic socks** (Thorlo brand, for example) that wick away the sweat and won't bunch up inside your boots. Avoid cotton, which is famous for causing blisters. Use moleskin or tape your most pesky problem places. (See the Foot Care section on page 17.)

Wear stretchy, comfortable **clothes** that allow you to move freely and won't bind when you're in a tuck position. Don't forget your sun protection, a full set of **protective gear,** and a good pair of **sunglasses** with large lenses.

For a workout over half an hour, carry enough water so you can sip a few ounces every 15 minutes. Use a **drinking system** that doesn't get in the way when you skate in a tuck. When planning to skate longer than an hour, pack an energy bar.

Whether you skate according to time or mileage, a properly calibrated **skate computer** can track both. A **heart rate monitor** allows you to track and adjust your training intensity midworkout.

Locations

Fitness skating requires a location where you can maintain a steady pace without interruption. Scour your neighborhoods for a convenient bike path that doesn't cross busy intersections, a back road with very little traffic, or a business park with streets that empty out after hours. A large, empty parking lot will do, too (see workout advice for a small area under Training Combinations, below). Hills are ideal for interval training.

Warm-Up, Stretching, and Cool-Down

Most people find an excuse to skip warming up, stretching, and cooling down, but they're probably unaware of the important fitness and injury prevention benefits, not the least of which is the reduction of postworkout muscle soreness.

Warm-Up

Warming up literally raises the temperature in your muscles, stimulates your nervous system, and lubricates your joints for easier skating. When you've properly warmed up, it takes longer to feel the burn in your muscles, because better blood flow from the start delays lactic acid buildup. To gradually increase your heart rate and prime your nervous system for skating, do some skills practice, one-foot drills, swizzle varieties, or just plain easy skating—all fun activities that stimulate your heart and blood flow. After 10 minutes, a light sweat or increased respiration indicates your muscles are now pliant enough to do a quick preworkout stretch.

Stretching

Relaxed, loose muscles make it easier to achieve a deeper tuck and a more powerful stroke while reducing the risk of muscle cramping, sprains, and strains. At a minimum, stretch your hip muscles, quadriceps, adductors, hamstrings, and lower back before and after skating. If you have time, add head tilts, shoulder shrugs, arm circles, side bends or rotations, and ankle rotations.

Arrange your body in the stretch position (see illustrations). Inhale and then begin to apply resistance (by pulling with your hands or using gravity or body weight). Take a long time to exhale, emptying your lungs by compressing your belly. Near the end of this first exhalation, you should be feeling a slight give in the stretching muscles. This is the point at which the muscle fibers release their protective reflex (usually 15–30 seconds) and a signal that you can now begin work to elongate them. Take another deep breath and exhale slowly, gently increasing the resistance.

Don't try stretching cold, because your muscles will resist and can actually tighten instead of lengthening. It is important that you perform all stretches *without* bouncing, which is likely to prolong the muscle's protective contraction and can also cause tiny tears in the tissue.

Lower back stretch. Raise shoulders until lower back stretches; avoid arching back unnaturally.

Inner thigh strengthener. Tighten buttocks and thighs and squat until thighs are at a right angle.

Back and groin stretch. With hands on shins, keep lower back straight and lean forward. Slide hands to ankles, and pull slightly forward, curving spine.

Calf stretch. With pelvis tucked forward and knee slightly bent, lean toward a support to stretch lower leg.

Quad stretch. Gripping a support with one hand, grasp a foot with the other and pull. Tuck pelvis forward for a better stretch.

Hamstring stretch. Grasp calf near ankle and pull gently. Flex foot to increase the stretch.

Stretches for skaters.

Cool-Down

A short post-skate cool-down reduces muscle soreness by flushing away exercise waste products. It also gives your heart some time to ease back to a more normal rate and stabilizes your circulation by recovering blood that has pooled in your arms and legs.

The most obvious way to cool down from hard skating is easy skating until you feel no signs of breathlessness. Now is a good time for a complete session of stretching, which earns you big couch potato points.

Key Skills

A well-rounded fitness skating program incorporates a solid stride as well as several beginners' skating skills. The workout techniques described below utilize the swizzle, half swizzles, scooters, and crossovers as described in chapter 2.

Don Kibler

Swizzles tone muscles and build strength.

Stride

To get the most benefit from your in-line workouts, you should have already mastered the drills described under Stride Technique in chapter 2. When doing roll aerobics,

- Concentrate on the elements of good stride technique on any route that safely allows fast, uninterrupted skating.

- Improve your capacity to store energy for short bursts of action by sprinting up a hill or on the flats until you become breathless.

- Improve balance and coordination by holding one long glide until you roll to a stop or begin to topple.

Forward Swizzles

Tracing hourglass figures on the pavement tones the hips and thighs while burning calories. Swizzling also enforces the lateral pushing and rear-wheel weight position, leading to more stroke power and efficiency. To use swizzles in a workout,

- Perform repeating sets of 30 swizzles to tone hips, thighs, and buttocks.

- Swizzle uphill to build power and stroking strength.

- Hold each swizzle's coiled squat for 8 counts, followed by two 4-count swizzles, to build muscular endurance.

Scooters

The scooter is nothing more than gliding on one skate while pushing off repeatedly with the other. Use scooters to

- Improve stroking efficiency by focusing on a lateral push and prolonging your heel contact with the pavement.

- Build outside edge balance and awareness by slightly tipping the support leg so you are gliding on the outside edge.

- Develop a speed skater's stride by doing scooters in an aerodynamic tuck with your nose and supporting knee aligned directly over the support skate.

Half Swizzles

To perform half swizzles, glide on one skate while swizzling repeatedly with the other. (You can also do half swizzles by alternating the half-swizzling skate right, left, right, left).

- Strengthen the stroke of your weak leg (yes, we all have one!) by doing half swizzles in a circle, with the weak leg doing all of the stroking. Rotate your head and upper body toward the center of the circle and glide on the inside skate while you pump the stroking skate in and out.

- Build muscular endurance by freezing the fully extended swizzling skate position for 8 counts. Repeat with the opposite leg.

- To improve balance and coordination, perform single or alternating half swizzles in slow motion.

Alternating Crossovers

This combination of stride and crossovers is done in a one-two-three rhythm: *right-glide, crossover, right-glide* followed by *left-glide, crossover, left-glide*. Because of the movement's zigzag path, a swath of pavement at least 15 feet wide is necessary. Keep your upper body facing forward. Use alternating crossovers in your workout to

- Strengthen both the pushing and pulling crossover muscles.

- Balance crossover technique to become equally proficient turning in both directions.

- Improve speed and cornering power by applying equal force to both the cross-under and crossover skate's push.

Training Combinations

Here are some suggested sequences for incorporating the above skills into a fitness skating program.

- Cycle repetitions of 20 swizzles, 20 alternating half swizzles, and 20 strides.

- Alternate sets of 20 fast-tempo strides with 20 long, slow strides.

- Perform repetitions of 1 minute of alternating half swizzles followed by 1 minute of alternating crossovers.

- Without changing legs, perform 20 fast scooters, followed by slow-motion scooters until the support leg is totally fatigued.

If you can't find a trail system or back road appropriate for skate fitness training, use the largest possible empty parking lot. Here are some training combinations for fitness skating in a compact space.

- Swizzle up and down the length of the parking lot for 15 minutes, alternating a lap of forward swizzles with one of half swizzles.

- Skate clockwise in a big circle, alternating five scooters with five half swizzles for 4 minutes or until the support leg is fatigued. Repeat in the opposite direction. Advanced skaters, try this using backward half swizzles.

- Tracing a large figure eight, skate one complete figure with crossovers and the next with half swizzles. Alternate for several figures; you'll have to switch the support leg where the two circles meet.

- Skating in a big circle, perform the following cycle of half swizzles: eight at regular speed, sixteen at double-time, and one held at full extension for several seconds. Repeat four times, then perform the same drill five times in the opposite direction.

While skating, check periodically to make sure you're within your training heart rate range (see below) by glancing at your heart rate monitor, if you have one, or by speaking a few words at a normal speaking rate, such as "Boy, am I getting a great workout today!" You should need to take a breath every three to four words. If you gasp several times before completing the sentence, slow down; if

ROLL MODEL

I started skating to cross train for skiing in 1988. After a brief stint with in-line racing, motherhood and injuries (*not* from skating) took me down another road—no more time to "train" the way I used to. That's when I realized the value of in-line skating . . . that the second I strapped on a pair I was doing great things for my body, at any intensity! For the next several years, I skated regularly.

That's my best fitness advice. Like me, you may not have tons of time to "train." It doesn't matter, because research says the most lasting effects of exercise occur with consistency. With light or heavy breathing, the simple action of striding is excellent for balance and conditioning the nervous system, which controls *every* function in the human body!

These days, my skate workouts have almost become ritualistic: "I've got to skate or I'll burn your dinner!" Just kidding, but I am serious about my skate time. I train so hard in so many other sports that I have reserved skating for my "peace-of-mind" workout (which is equally as important as the kick-my-butt cardio burn). Benton Crossing Road represents my favorite workout location . . . a 50-mile, meandering two-lane road on the outskirts of Mammoth Lakes. Hardly any traffic . . . it's just me, the cows, wind, and mountains on crystal clear pavement. I thank God for being able to skate in a postcard every day!

—Suzanne Nottingham, IISA Inline Certification Program Examiner, coauthor of *Fitness In-Line Skating,* and nationally known fitness expert

Heart rate training.

you can say the entire phrase with one breath, increase the intensity by skating faster, choosing a harder skill, flexing into a deeper position, or actively engaging your arms in the movement.

Heart Rate Training

Monitoring your heart rate during a workout tells you exactly how hard you're working and whether you are on track with your training goals. A heart rate monitor is the best way to accomplish this because its feedback capabilities help you stay within your desired range.

In order to establish the ranges you will use for training, you must first determine your own maximum heart rate (MHR) and your anaerobic threshold (AT). (Definitions for these two terms are in this chapter's Dialect sidebar.)

Maximum Heart Rate

The standard way to determine your maximum heart rate is to subtract your age from 220 if you are male, and from 226 if you are female. The resulting value is really only a predicted "normal" estimate based on other people's bodies. Not knowing your own actual MHR could lead to under- or over-training, so it's best to determine the actual number.

The safest method for finding out your maximum heart rate is to set up an appointment for a monitored test through your doctor. This is especially advisable for beginning and intermediate fitness skaters. And there is no guarantee that an elite athlete can self-test without experiencing negative health consequences.

If you own a heart rate monitor and are supremely confident in your cardiovascular health, go to a health club that has treadmills. For the most accurate results, be sure to take a rest day beforehand.

Wearing your heart rate monitor, warm up for 15 minutes. Then, slightly increase your effort every 2 minutes by setting a higher speed or raising the treadmill's incline level. When you reach a point at which you know you absolutely must quit (your arms hurt and your vision becomes blurry), quickly make note of your heart rate and set the treadmill to a slow, flat, cool-down/recovery mode. You've now recorded your maximum heart rate.

Anaerobic Threshold

To *estimate* your anaerobic threshold, subtract 20 from your maximum heart rate. To find your true AT, get back on that treadmill wearing your heart rate monitor. Slowly increase the workload until you reach the highest pace you can maintain for 20 minutes (it should feel very difficult but doable).

After 15 minutes at this pace, start watching your heart rate and complete the 20-minute session. The average heart rate during the last 5 minutes is your AT, a value in beats per minute.

Typically, untrained individuals reach AT at 70 to 75 percent of MHR, while elite athletes can remain aerobic until 85 to 90 percent. To determine the heart rate percentage where your own AT falls, use the formula $(AT/MHR) \times 100 = nn\%$. Training hard just below your calculated AT actually raises your anaerobic threshold, meaning you'll be able to work harder and longer before lactic acid begins to burn in your muscles.

Using myself as an example, with a maximum heart rate of 190, I've determined that 170 beats per minute is my anaerobic threshold. When doing distance training to raise my AT, I use my heart rate monitor to make sure it reads a consistent 168–170. At this pace I'm feeling quite breathless but able to keep up the work. A skater new to fitness training may feel the same way with a heart rate of 140 beats per minute.

Chart Your Own Training Rates

Make a copy of the table below to log your maximum heart rate, current anaerobic threshold, and beats per minute for the various training goals in the Per Minute column. The RPE column represents Rate of Perceived Exertion to help you assess workout intensity without a heart rate monitor.

	Per Min.	RPE	Training Use
MHR (100%)		10—can't continue	Establish maximum heart rate
95%		9—very, very hard	Anaerobic intervals to increase energy reserves for short bursts (speed skating breakaways, sprints, steep climbs)
90%		8—very, very hard	Anaerobic intervals to raise AT (which determines the onset of lactic acid buildup)
85%		7—very hard	Anaerobic intervals; muscular endurance and strength training
AT		(very hard)	AT training (at the lactate threshold) to improve aerobic fitness via long, steady workouts. This heart rate ranges anywhere from 70 to 90% of MHR depending on the individual.
80%		6—fairly hard	Aerobic training for cardio fitness; aerobic interval training for muscular endurance
75%		5—light	Aerobic training for cardio fitness and fat burning
70%		4—very light	Recovery and fat burning

Plan Your Program

Setting Goals

Setting realistic, measurable goals makes a big impact on your success in any endeavor, including fitness. You'll be more likely to remain focused until you meet your goals when you've set them, written them down, and shared them with a friend. For starters, establish a short-range goal for your cardio fitness. A very specific and measurable example would be *I want to be able to skate from point A to point B in X minutes while maintaining a heart rate within Y, my aerobic training zone.*

A monthly, 30-minute, point-to-point time trial such as this makes a great self-test to track the effectiveness of your fitness program, no matter what your skating level or goals.

If fat loss is part of the plan, a specific goal might be *I want to lose X pounds of body fat and still have the muscle to do X push-ups by MM/DD/YY.*

If you're a speed skater training for a big event on a certain day, you will require a series of short- and midrange fitness goals to gradually build up your fitness on multiple fronts.

Training Cycles

Training cycles let you focus on specific fitness improvements that evolve according to a planned time span. Gear your fitness goals toward a specific date at which you plan to be at peak performance level, whether it's the day of an important race or a personal fitness deadline.

In conjunction with cardio work, start your skate fitness program by easing into resistance training to build the structural strength that allows you to maintain balance and good form while skating. Once you have this solid foundation, design a series of workouts that gradually become harder as the weeks pass.

- Exercise at increasingly higher heart rates when doing aerobics or distance skating to gradually improve cardiovascular fitness.

- Skate "very hard" to introduce aerobic in-

If your in-line fitness goal is to	Refer to
Decrease body fat or increase calorie consumption	Cardiovascular endurance, p. 48 Performance nutrition, p. 53
Improve cardiovascular health	Cardiovascular endurance, p. 48
Tone and firm abdomen, hips, lower back, and thighs	Muscular strength, p. 49 Swizzles and half swizzles, pp. 42–43
Build endurance for a skate tour or long-distance skate event	Cardiovascular endurance, p. 48 Muscular endurance, p. 49 Swizzles and half swizzles, pp. 42–43 Interval training, p. 48
Improve power for sprints, hill climbing, or race breakaways	Power stride, pp. 23–28 Interval training, p. 48
Improve performance in other sports or give skating muscles a break	Cross training, p. 50
Train for speed skating competitions	A phased multiweek training cycle in the following sequence: aerobic fitness, muscular endurance, muscular strength, intervals, and plyometrics. See Race Training, p. 99

tervals to your workouts to improve tolerance of lactic acid buildup.

- Start adding "very, very hard" sprints and uphill work to introduce anaerobic intervals that can increase energy reserves for short bursts of work.

- Involve more muscle groups when resistance training; increase the load while decreasing the rest periods to build muscular strength and endurance.

- **Advanced:** Add weekly plyometric training sessions on your off days to develop explosive power, gradually working up to twice a week performing hops and bounds immediately after resistance training sessions. (Save this for next year if you're new to fitness work.)

Predesigned, cyclic workouts to suit the needs of every skater are detailed in an easy-to-follow format in the book *Fitness In-Line Skating* by experts Suzanne Nottingham and Frank Fedel. The book *Speed on Skates* by Canadian speed coach Barry Publow provides excellent advice for designing your own cyclic training plan.

Charting Your Plan

However you build your workout week, an effective performance-improving program needs to include some combination of the following elements.

- **Cardiovascular endurance:** One to two hours of aerobics three times per week (cross train without skates at least once); vary times, distances, and intensity throughout the week

- **Intervals:** Up to two hours of timed intervals, sprints, or hill climbs; one session each per week at first, building to two sessions

SUNDAY	MONDAY	TUESDAY	WEDNESDAY	THURSDAY	FRIDAY	SATURDAY
21 Intervals	22 Weights/Plyometrics	23 Cardio	24 Recovery (very light cross train)	25 Intervals	26 Weights	27 Cardio/AT Training

SUNDAY	MONDAY	TUESDAY	WEDNESDAY	THURSDAY	FRIDAY	SATURDAY
7 Intervals	8 Cardio	9 Weights	10 Cardio/AT Training	11 Weights	12 Cardio/Cross Training	13 Recovery
14 Cardio	15 Weights	16 Cardio/AT Training	17 Recovery	18 Cardio	19 Weights	20 Intervals

Top: Sample endurance program. **Bottom:** Sample speed program.

- **Aerobic threshold training:** One session per week, building from 15 minutes of light effort to very hard for the last 2–3 minutes of effort at your AT

- **Resistance training:** Two to three times per week, not on aerobic days

- **Plyometrics** (advanced athletes only): Once a week in a dedicated session when just starting, added to end of a resistance training session later

- **Recovery days:** Once or twice per week (light aerobics or no training at all)

A sample two-week endurance program and a one-week speed program incorporating the above elements are charted on page 47.

Training Focus

When it comes right down to it, the quality and quantity of your workouts are determining factors in your performance on skates. There are as many training routines as there are skaters, but they all should include cardiovascular work, interval training, and resistance training. Whether or not you have another active sport that complements your skating, include cross training days to prevent overuse injuries and boredom.

The following descriptions are overviews only. See the Fitness Resources section at the end of this chapter for a list of books and other materials where you can find comprehensive information and training advice.

Cardiovascular Endurance

It is important that you strengthen your heart as well as the rest of your muscles. At the maintenance level, your weekly fitness program should already include some activity that sustains an aerobic heart rate for at least 25 minutes three times per week. But to actually improve your aerobic fitness level, you need to increase these sessions to a minimum of six days per week.

You can improve aerobic fitness with ex-

tended periods of uninterrupted skating at 60–90 percent of your maximum heart rate. Skating intervals can do this, too: short, intense bursts of anaerobic effort interspersed with rest periods. Besides better cardiovascular performance, secondary benefits from your cardio training include a lower resting heart rate, improved skate-specific muscular endurance, and a higher utilization of fat for energy.

Interval Training

To really improve your body's capacity to process oxygen, add interval training sessions. These consist of short spurts of work performed at about 90 percent of your MHR followed by a measured rest period and then repeated. Before you begin adding interval sessions, build up to them with a solid six weeks of aerobic workouts totaling no less than four to five hours a week.

To introduce intervals, swap one aerobic workout per week with an interval training session over three to four weeks, after which you can increase your interval training days to two. Be sure to take a rest or skate at a recovery level the day following interval training. Skip all interval work once every four to five weeks to avoid overtraining.

Interval training alternates repeated bouts of intensive activity with timed spans of slower periods of the same activity. This active rest time allows the blood flow to flush lactic acid away from the muscles. Warm up by skating easily on flat terrain for at least 5 minutes. Ideally, the sets of intensive skating (or biking, running, etc.) should raise your heart rate to 85 to 95 percent of maximum for 1 to 4 minutes. Follow immediately with recovery periods, where you settle down to a low aerobic training rate for three times as long as the interval lasted. Try to work up to three or four interval/recovery sets per session. If you can continue an interval beyond 5 minutes or it does not make you breathless, increase the intensity. Because every body is different, you will probably need to experiment with work and rest times, distances, and the number of repetitions to identify a strategy that suits your individual needs.

Strength Training

A well-planned strength training program improves the body's general flexibility, muscular strength, and muscular endurance. Added muscle mass results in better power output, increased energy for intense activities, and a metabolism that burns more calories. Resistance training helps maintain total body fitness and improves your ability to recover positively from bouts of hard exercise.

Ease slowly into strength training to avoid muscle soreness and joint injuries. If you've never done this before, enlist the help of a personal fitness trainer and learn proper lifting techniques for both free weights and machines. Start with a month of just two workouts per week, doing 15 easy reps of the following exercises.

- bench presses (chest, shoulders, and triceps)
- behind the neck pull-downs (back and biceps)
- crunches (abdomen)
- back extensions (lower back)
- leg presses (thighs and buttocks)

Always warm up before strength training and wait 48 hours between sessions to allow full recovery. Once you've gotten used to the weights and learned safe lifting technique, start incorporating training methods that build endurance, strength, and power.

Muscular endurance: To improve your muscles' capacity to repetitively perform the same movement without fatigue, increase your strength training sessions to three times per week. Work the trunk and lower body muscles every session and work the upper back, chest, and arms once a week. Select a resistance for each exercise that allows you to perform two or three sets of 30 to 40 slow controlled reps in good form, with the last repetition

a near failure. Take 2 seconds to lift and 3 to lower the weight. Rest no more than 90 seconds between sets.

Muscular strength: To build greater stroke power and acceleration capabilities, perform strength training up to three times a week using exercises that work the gluteals, hip flexors, quadriceps, hamstrings, abductors, and adductors. Continue to work the upper back, chest, and arms once a week. For trunk work, include crunches (strong abs help reduce lower back pain in a tuck) and back extensions to strengthen your spinal erectors. To build strength, select a resistance for each exercise that allows you to perform three sets of 10 to 12 reps in good form, with the last repetition a near failure. Lower the weight slowly and rest no more than 2 minutes between sets.

Muscular power (plyometrics): To gain greater sprinting speed or power for that extra kick when climbing a hill, add exercises that result in explosive muscular contractions. Off-skate plyometric training utilizes hopping, bounding, and jumping movements. The plyometric moves that contribute to skating power are lateral step-ups, sideways hops over a knee-high bench, forward broad jumps, and one-footed hops in a forward zigzagging path.

Delay introducing plyometric drills until you have sufficiently built up your tendons and muscles through resistance training to withstand the high impact forces. Avoid plyometric training altogether if indicated by your age, current fitness level, or injury history (when in doubt, check with your family doctor or a personal trainer who knows you well). A spinning bike or a slide board are good alternatives for building explosiveness.

To avoid injury, wear a pair of supportive aerobic or cross training shoes to protect against the high impacts of plyometrics. Warm up thoroughly with light aerobics, stretching, and very easy versions of the exercises to be performed. Incorporate the exercises slowly into your workouts, starting with a separate weekly session and gradually building to a level where you can add them at the end of a resistance training workout.

Step-Ups

One-Foot Zigzag Hops

Lateral High Hops

Two-Foot Zigzag Hops

Plyometric training involves intense, anaerobic intervals. (Adapted from Chu, *Jumping into Plyometrics*)

A thorough, well-illustrated guide on this topic for fitness and speed skaters is *Strength and Power Training for Speedskaters*, by Barry Publow. See the Fitness Resources section at the end of this chapter.

Cross Training Alternatives

Almost every move you make on skates will result in a fall if you get out of balance. The more time you spend skating and the more skills you master, the better your balance becomes. The constant, semiconscious adjustments you make to stay on your feet not only keep you balanced but translate to better overall coordination, a benefit that applies to all other physical activities. That's why so many competitive athletes from other sports turn to in-line skating for cross training.

Apply your heightened balance, timing, and coordination to your favorite nonskating forms of exercise and recreation. For dedicated fitness or competitive skaters, cross training provides a refreshing mind break from sport-specific training and reduces boredom or the chance of burnout. You'll use different muscles while your skating muscles rest and recover, reducing the risk of overuse injury. A little cross training variety also results in a well-rounded fitness lifestyle, no matter who you are or what your goals.

Aerobics Classes

For in-line cross training, it's important to get consistent workouts that meet your conditioning goals and offer enough variety to prevent overuse injuries. Indoor aerobic machines and classes such as spinning, step aerobics, and martial arts sessions offer plenty of on- and off-season variety for maintaining and improving cardiovascular and muscular fitness, coordination, and flexibility. But when there's fresh air and smooth pavement available, get outdoors and enjoy nature for your workout, because this also exercises your soul!

Alpine Skiing

Downhill skiing is almost as beneficial to in-line skating as slalom skating is to skiing. Turning, edging, weight transfer, and balance are very similar in both sports. Because the same muscles are used, skiing during the winter keeps you in shape for skating once the snow has melted, and vice versa. On skis, repeated high-intensity spurts of activity translate to an effective form of interval training. On skates, skating back uphill for another run adds to the training workload. After a season of properly executed slalom turns on skates, it's much easier to maintain the flexed, centered position over the ski's sweet spot that is so essential to turning and control, even when faced with moguls and steeps.

Snowboarders also achieve complementary cross training benefits with in-line skating; both sports involve excellent balance and whole-body coordination. See chapter 5 if you're an alpine ski enthusiast.

Cross-Country Skiing

Cross-country skiing has long been known as the ultimate aerobic conditioning sport because its "high rep–low weight" repetitions involve large muscles in both the upper and lower body. The rhythmic kick and glide are reminiscent of in-line's stride and glide. When done on specialized skating skis, the skier's lateral push from inside edges is very close to a skater's power stride, both of which result in forward momentum.

Whether you're on skate-style skis, in-lines, or roller skis, the same herringbone (toes-out) position is used to climb, and the workout is equally taxing on all three types of equipment. For both snow and pavement, ski poles are an asset to hill climbing. For dry-land training, use rubber-tipped ski poles on paved trails to involve your upper body muscles and more closely replicate the wintertime workout.

Cycling

Road and mountain biking are both great for improving your balance on in-line skates. The lateral weight shift that results in a banked turn on a bike is not unlike that of a parallel or crossover turn on skates. Biking strengthens the muscles of the lower body (buttocks, hamstrings, quadriceps, and calves) and gives them better staying power for long training sessions. These are the same muscles used for skating, but biking stimulates them in a different way, making the two sports highly complementary. The cyclist's low-over-the-handlebars position and the speed skater's tuck position are similar enough to enhance training benefits. From the cyclist's point of view, skating uphill works all the lower body muscles that directly apply to speed on a bicycle.

For convenience or as a bad weather alternative, there's always the local gym with its fleet of stationary bikes, complete with heart rate monitors.

Ice Skating

If you can get access to free-skate time on an ice rink, consider taking up ice skating, which mimics in-line movements. For the first-timer, the ice will feel alarmingly slick compared to pavement, and you might have to stick to the sidelines for a couple of laps. But once your confidence allows you to skate in a relaxed ready position, you should be able to do almost everything you can do on in-lines except stop with a heel brake.

Indoor in-line racers should cross train on the ice if possible. A precise stroke is more important here, because the blade is so narrow and flat, with the inside and outside edges very close together. The longer glide time on ice eventually results in better one-footed balance and hip stability.

Rowing

The arm swings that enhance the skater's hill climbing power or starting line sprints use the muscles in the shoulders, arms, and upper back. These are the same muscles developed by rowing. This activity also contributes to all-round athletic fitness, balancing out the many lower body muscles that skating develops.

Thanks to the ready availability of indoor rowing machines in fitness clubs, anybody can benefit from rowing. Outdoors, rowing is a stimulating al fresco workout. In many waterside cities, it's possible to participate in regular crew sessions using the sponsoring organization's equipment. Sea kayaking is another, more adventurous water sport that stimulates development of the muscles in the upper body and aids in balance development.

Dan Kibler

Off-skates cross training.

Running

Running is one fitness activity that is even more convenient than in-line skating, because it requires only a good pair of running shoes and a sturdy lower body. It's an effective way to work on your muscular and cardiovascular endurance while offering a nice change of pace from skating. From the opposite point of view, if you're a serious runner, a day of skating—whether you go fast and hard or keep it at a recovery pace—is a welcome break for the knees. It also strengthens your hill climbing muscles, the glutes and quads.

Running is best suited to younger bodies: Anybody with a volatile lower back or a history of joint problems in the hips, knees, or ankles should steer clear of this high-impact form of exercise. The likelihood of such structural problems and injuries increases with age, as does the tendency to gain a few extra pounds, which only adds to the stress of running.

Tennis

Tennis is ideal for improving your ability to make quick starts and stops and sudden direction changes. These are the same skills in-line hockey players use. The legs are constantly in play, and the body position when receiving a serve is the same as the in-line skater's ready position: loosely upright and flexed at the hips, knees, and ankles. Tennis's need for speed and good peripheral vision apply directly to a fast-moving game of hockey.

Walking

If walking was your favorite aerobic activity before you took up skating, don't hesitate to shed the wheels and substitute a vigorous stroll, which makes an ideal recovery day. The low-impact, aerobic benefits of a brisk stride have long been proven. With walking, the stress factor is very low because beautiful surroundings are easier to admire at a slower pace.

Other cross-training candidates not covered here (horseback riding, yoga, even race-car driving, to cite the histories of a few of my students) may also stimulate the balance, strength, endurance, and discipline that applies directly to fitness skating success.

A healthy dinner plate.

Performance Nutrition

It's important to eat a healthy diet that supports your fitness goals rather than hindering them. This starts at your local grocery store. Do your best to fill your shopping cart with unprocessed, highly nutritional foods, leaving out packaged and canned goods as much as possible. There should be no room in that cart for sweet and salty junk foods such as chips and pastries. Instead, load up with fresh fish, low-fat meat and dairy products, soy-based proteins, almonds, fruit, and munchable raw vegetables. While you're in the produce section, add a variety of greens and squashes, mushrooms, avocados, and tomatoes. Buy high quality sprouted-grain breads and whole wheat fat-free tortillas but avoid full-size bagels and other starchy grains. Refresh your stocks of soy sauce, garlic, onions, olive oil, and fresh herbs to add flavor when cooking.

Try to save eating out for special occasions. Daily or even weekly trips to restaurants and fast food outlets make it difficult to control both the quantity and quality of your intake. Even with the demands of a major fitness training program, more and more studies are proving that a restricted-calorie lifestyle actually prolongs the average life span. To maintain daylong energy reserves, eat small meals for breakfast, lunch, and dinner (don't skip!) and smaller snacks two or three times a day, so you never go more than four hours without food. Waiting six to eight hours between feedings invariably results in eating more than your body needs, not to mention wide swings in your blood sugar level, which can hurt both the body's insulin management system and your energy level.

The Carbo Controversy

I've been successfully following the Zone diet since late 1997. Besides allowing me to stay lean by tapping into stored body fat when I need energy, eating this way lets me wake up energized every morning, and on an hour less sleep than I used to need. Using the Zone nutrient ratios, 40 percent of each meal's calories come from nonstarchy carbohydrates (fresh fruits and vegetables), 30 percent from low-fat protein and 30 percent from fat, mostly monounsaturated. I never get sleepy after eating because I avoid the typical large servings of pasta, rice, or potatoes. Eating this way keeps my blood sugar even all day long, whether I'm working at my computer, skiing the black diamond runs, or doing a 20-mile skate. I've also gotten a lot stronger in the gym. And yes, sometimes I cheat, but it's easy to reenter the Zone at my next meal.

Unfortunately, because today's athletes have come to depend on a high carbohydrate diet and the USDA food guide pyramid has gained such prominence in America, the 40/30/30 concept of eating is a too-controversial paradigm shift for most people. The only way to find out if eating a natural foods Zone diet will improve your own overall performance, strength, and energy reserves is to try it for yourself. It sure works for me!

FITNESS RESOURCES

PUBLICATIONS

Fitness In-Line Skating. Suzanne Nottingham and Frank Fedel. Champaign IL: Human Kinetics, 1997.

Jumping into Plyometrics: 100 Exercises for Power and Strength. Donald A. Chu. Champaign IL: Human Kinetics, 1998.

Skate Fit: The Complete In-Line Skating Workout. Bradley, Carolyn. New York: ABA Inc., 1994.

Speed on Skates: A Complete Technique, Training, and Racing Guide for In-Line and Ice Skaters. Barry Publow. Champaign IL: Human Kinetics, 1999.

Strength and Power Training for Speedskaters. Barry Publow. Ottawa: Breakaway Speed Specialists; 1998.

The Zone: A Dietary Road Map. Barry Sears and William Lawren. New York: HarperCollins, 1995.

VIDEOS

Rollerdancing: A Workout on Skates. Richard Humphrey. San Francisco: Movement in Motion Productions, 1995, 415-469-0909.

WEBSITES

<www.rollerblade.com> Launched with a 14-city tour in 1999, Rollerblade, Inc.'s BladeFitness Program offers aerobics classes on wheels designed to be a fun and social group workout. The program brings together local retailers who help with promotion and health clubs who supply facilities and specially trained fitness instructors.

CHAPTER FOUR

In-Line Touring

DIALECT

bicycle route: Designated roadway where bicycles are allowed to share the right-of-way with motor vehicles; identified by signs.

bike lane: Portion of a roadway designated for one-way bike travel, identified by bike route signs, lane striping, and other pavement markings.

bike path: A completely separate right-of-way dedicated exclusively for the use of nonmotorized travel.

FNS: Commonly used acronym for Friday Night Skate, a weekly group skate.

scissors stance: A defensive posture used to ride over irregular or rough pavement. Coasting with one skate a boot length ahead of the other and feet in a narrow stance results in a longer wheel base that improves stability for managing gravel, grass, manhole covers, wood slat bridges, and all varieties of rough paving.

(continued on next page)

Something's up in the city, and the buzz of anticipation is almost tangible. It's approaching dusk as the transformation begins. The ripping sound of Velcro draws the attention to skaters gearing up next to their cars. Wheeled folks clutching water bottles weave among pedestrians on the sidewalks, all flowing toward the same destination. Some stroke along purposefully; others chatter and laugh excitedly. Before long, 100, 800, 2,000 in-line skaters have converged at the designated meeting place!

Crazy costumes and fancy footwork catch the eye. Skating buddies find each other while others chat with strangers joined by the bond of skating. Suddenly the call to roll pierces the evening air. A cheer erupts as the party begins to spin off into the night like some undulating, thousand-wheeled organism. In its wake, the city gapes in amazement.

In-line skating is a unique and satisfying way to experience a new city, region, or culture, because it blends the stop-and-look flexibility of walking with the mobility of wheels. As skating skill and confidence grow, the itch to explore begins its magnetic pull, drawing those with an adventurous spirit beyond their familiar environs to wherever their wheels might take them.

Touring Near and Far

In-line touring is a versatile form of active recreation that costs nothing after the initial investment and can be enjoyed anywhere there's smooth pavement. It's a great form of family recreation because people of all ages enjoy it. And it's very safe, as long as you're fully protected by a helmet and other protective gear, pay keen attention to your surroundings, and let others know you're there.

> **DIALECT** *(continued from previous page)*
>
> **skitching:** Skating + hitching; the very dangerous practice of grabbing onto a car to hitch a ride. Don't do it if you want to avoid injury!
>
> **stroller skating:** Skating a trail while pushing a baby stroller.

Something for Everyone

You don't have to be an expert or superfit to enjoy a tour on skates. You develop the right skills little by little each time you venture out for a roll in a new location or situation. You can safely approach in-line touring in the following sequence.

1. Skating on vehicle-free bike paths within (and later outside) the local community

2. Using designated commuter-oriented bike lanes on the edges of city streets

3. Joining a group skate or big-city "Friday Night Skate" (required skills vary)

4. Signing up for multiday guided group tours in North America or overseas (Zephyr Inline Skate Tours takes all skill levels—see the Touring Resources section at the end of this chapter.)

5. Exploring low-traffic back roads (see Scouting New Routes, below)

Dedicated Paths

We live in a fortunate age. Every year, more and more communities, park districts, and neighborhood developers expand their trail networks to provide citizens with greater opportunities to commute or exercise on traffic-free pathways.

To find new places to skate, ask the employees of skate or bike shops or get a copy of the town's bicycle transportation map and look for bike paths dedicated to nonmotorized users.

Individual skaters across North America have published descriptions of their favorite routes in books and on the Internet. I researched 300 California destinations in 1995 for *California In-Line Skating: The Complete Guide to the Best Places to Skate*. See the Touring Resources section for information on this and other available directories.

Bike Lanes

Bike lanes offer the easiest transition from dedicated paths to street skating. Because the roadside striping and other lane markings usually follow a town's common commuter routes, they're great for getting around to run errands or roll to work.

Make sure you are up to date on the local ordinances and know to what level they are enforced upon skaters. Fortunately, in most communities in-lines are allowed simply because they aren't specifically prohibited. Contact your local National Skate Patrol (if your town has one), active

Dan Kibler

Touring the local bike path.

skate club, or bicycle transportation agency for more information. When skating on multiuse dedicated paths, obey the Rules of the Road (see page 59) and be considerate of other trail users.

In the bike lanes, you share the same responsibilities as bicyclists, including skating on the right side with the flow of traffic. Try to stay within the striped lines when possible, but realize that you also have the right to adequate road width to react safely to the sudden appearance of obstacles or unforeseen situations. Use deliberate eye contact and hand signals to make your intentions and expectations clear to motorists.

To avoid confusing motorists and thereby endangering yourself, stay in the bike lanes rather than switching back and forth from the road (behaving like a cyclist) to the sidewalk (behaving like a pedestrian), especially at busy intersections.

Wearing a helmet and the rest of the protective gear is not only a good safety precaution but also alerts drivers to the fact that you are moving much faster than pedestrian speed. This reduces the risk of a motorist suddenly cutting across your path to make a right turn.

Back Roads

SCOUTING NEW ROUTES

Despite the absence of bike lanes, well-chosen, low-traffic roads can be perfect for touring. The best way to find good and safe countryside skate routes is to research the area by car first. Seek out a back road that would be good for an out-and-back run, a loop, or skating to a shuttle vehicle at the end. Stop briefly on the roadside every couple of miles and check the pavement quality and debris factor. If the route is over 20 miles long, scout out a likely picnic location and make note of where you can find a rest room or fresh water. Skate the route to see if it warrants a repeat.

When predicting the amount of use a road gets, painted-on markings are a good indicator of traffic density. Roads with no painted lines serve the smallest number of vehicles and are best for skaters. The next best are those with a single white

Skating on roadside bike lanes.

Dan Kibler

line down the middle. Yellow lines indicate more daily traffic—avoid these. Find out the traffic patterns at different times of the day or week.

SKATING IN THE ROAD

If you aren't sure of an area's roadway codes, find out what activities are considered illegal and to what extent they are enforced.

As long as skating isn't specifically forbidden, if there is no marked shoulder you can travel on the road in the direction of traffic. In this wilder skating environment, pay extra attention to the road surface and watch out for loose gravel or other debris in driveways. Stay to the right and, if the road is narrow, stop stroking when a car approaches from behind so it has room to pass safely. Mind the foot closest to traffic: You don't want to get clipped.

Some of the best slalom skating is found on sloped country roads or in quiet hillside neighborhoods. It's okay to use the whole lane to make speed-cutting turns on steep hills, as long as you don't obstruct traffic (wait for all traffic to pass before you start down). Once you have made the choice to occupy a lane, hold your ground until you can safely return to the right, but don't allow the situation to force you into going faster than your abilities allow.

If you do slalom training on a road with blind corners, arrange to have somebody follow in a car to control the traffic behind you. If you know a group of willing bicyclists, enlist at least four as escorts for such a location, with two spanning your lane in front and two in back.

For serious adventurers or cross-country travelers, point-to-point touring is a more challenging form of back-road skating. The well-outfitted adventurer starts at point A and uses a map to skate to point B without having previously researched every mile. This method presents the problems of carrying more gear and hitting unexpected road surfaces or traffic conditions. If maps and multiday exploring sound appealing but you'd rather not deal with the burdens of self-support, see Guided Tours later in this chapter.

Metro Group Skates

Participating in group rolls is one of the best ways to build confidence and street skills. Since many group skates take place at dusk or after dark, be sure you know the terrain and pavement quality in advance. Call the contact person (or check the group's Web site) to get an idea of the distance, hills, and pavement quality. Your best bet after dark is to follow in the tracks of somebody who is a regular on the route while making your own mental notes for the next trip.

Depending on the route, the city's tolerance level, and the number of participants, it is often possible to temporarily take over an entire lane of the road or street. In these cases, stay on the right side of the street and avoid blocking the flow of traffic whenever possible.

When the route includes traffic lights, obey all signals unless the organizers have taken control of the intersection. Comply with any instructions from police organizers or Skate Patrollers and try not to lag behind the crowd.

SAFETY IN A CROWD

- Wear full armor! The more people there are around you, the more likely that somebody is going to trip you.

- Skate within *your* abilities, not those of the pack leaders or the skater ahead of you.

- Look over your shoulder before making a sudden swerve.

- Resist skating slalom style down a hill in a crowd.

- Behave predictably around motorists and don't assume they will see or accommodate you.

- Don't skitch. If you can't make it up a hill under your own power, you have no business participating.

- Don't skate under the influence of drugs or alcohol.

- Keep all your senses tuned so you can quickly respond to sudden changes in your environment. Keep watch on the road surface and upcoming terrain and constantly check right and left for cars or other surprises. Never wear headphones, which can drown out danger signals.

- After dark, wear white, add reflective material to gear and clothing, and wear flashing lights or headlamps to increase your visibility.

Guided Tours

The ultimate in-line touring experience is an active sightseeing vacation where a tour operator handles travel logistics (meals, lodging, and luggage transfers) while you take a daily premapped roll through new territory at your own pace.

Since the spring of 1997, Minnesota-based Zephyr Inline Skate Tours, Inc., has offered a growing variety of tours to suit all levels of ability. Itineraries includes several North American destinations (Amish country and Martha's Vine-

RULES OF THE ROAD

Every skater should adopt good trail etiquette and safety habits. The following "rules" are distributed by the International Inline Skating Association and taught by its certified instructors.

SKATE SMART

- Always wear your helmet, wrist guards, and knee and elbow pads.
- Learn the basics: speed control, turning, braking, and stopping.
- Keep all your equipment in safe condition.

SKATE LEGAL

- Observe all traffic regulations; on skates, you must obey the laws for wheeled vehicles.
- Skate with, not against, the flow of traffic.
- Don't "skitch." Never allow yourself to be towed by a motorized vehicle or bicycle.

SKATE ALERT

- Always skate in control.
- Stay away from water, oil, debris, sand, and uneven or broken pavement.
- Avoid areas with heavy traffic.
- Avoid wearing headphones or anything that makes it hard to hear.

SKATE POLITE

- Skate on the right side of the path and call out a warning before you pass on the left ("Passing your left!").
- Yield to pedestrians.
- Stop stroking to make room for passing cyclists (and avoid catching a skate in their spokes!).
- Be a goodwill ambassador for in-line skating.

---

yard, to name two) and trips to the Netherlands, Switzerland, and the most popular European FNS locations. Each day, the in-line tourists choose from three routes of differing lengths, deciding for themselves how far or how little they want to skate. A support van waits at various points along the way, offering the chance to swap to an alternate pair of skates, grab a snack, or hitch a ride. Skaters take in the scenic routes and culture at their own pace or in small groups rather than in one large group. The guides are qualified instructors dedicated to making sure each customer has a fun, trouble-free trip and has every opportunity to become a more skilled skater.

Nothing tops in-line touring as a way to ex-plore the world, make new friends, and improve your technique, all at the same time. Look for more opportunities and destinations emerge as the number of people who take up the in-line lifestyle expands.

Key Skills

Stroke Technique

Although you can manage most tours and group skates with a basic stride, the more efficient and powerful stride technique described in chapter 2 is your key to enjoying mile after mile of almost ef-fortless skating.

Handling the Unpredictable

No matter what the route, potholes, train or tram tracks, rough pavement, debris, puddles, street grates, manhole covers, raised roots, and sidewalk slabs are all possibilities when you're touring. You'll be more likely to appreciate the scenery if you are competent in the following skills:

- heel brake stop (pages 28–30)
- scissors stance coasting (page 28)
- anticipation (page 23)
- speed control (page 30)
- street skills (page 23)
- uphill skating (page 31)

WHEN THE PAVEMENT IS WET

An extended day's tour might put you in a situation where you're far from shelter when a rainsquall hits. To skate on wet surfaces, shorten the length of each stroke by up to 50 percent to keep your feet closer under your hips and the wheels more upright on the pavement. Make light, fast strokes but make sure you fully shift your weight directly over the gliding support skate to reduce the chance of losing your balance if (when) the stroking wheels lose grip.

Avoid crossover turns, because the tilt moves your center of gravity away from the support leg, which is likely to cause wheel slippage. Stopping will require more distance, whether you're dragging wheels in a T-stop or using a heel brake.

Fitness

Plain and simple, the more fit you are, the more you'll enjoy skate touring, no matter what type you do. If you're planning a long one-day excursion or a multiday tour, start shaping up far enough in advance to be prepared for the planned mileage.

On a vacation-style skate tour, expect to be skating a minimum of 10 and up to 40 miles a day, if you choose. If that is beyond your current capabilities, design a skating workout to gradually increase your mileage starting several weeks—if not months—ahead of time.

To prevent muscle soreness and charley horses, warm up for 5 minutes and stretch your legs, back, and hips prior to a long day's skate. Afterwards, spend another 10 minutes on a full stretch. Your muscles will thank you. See chapter 3 for detailed fitness advice.

Packing for a Day Trip

Generally, you'll be most comfortable using the smallest pack possible to meet the purpose of any given trip. Depending on the intended distance and the weather (and what gear you own), this could mean anything from stuffing the pouches of a pair of cargo shorts to loading up a day pack, a fanny pack, or the pockets of a hydration system.

Skates, Wheels, and Bearings

Fitness skates are your best bet for daylong distance skating over variable surfaces (see an excellent model by Salomon on page 39). If you already own a pair of skates that remain comfortable after several hours and miles, bring them. If not, remember

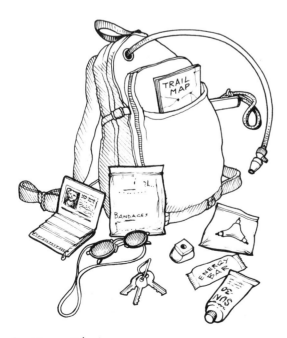

Day trip essentials.

ROLL MODEL

With our cultural sensitivity heightened by Zephyr's introductory talk, we set out for the day's adventure. We were skating to Medemblik and back. After skating through Andijk—on bricks, of course—we climbed up to the top of the dike where we would spend most of the rest of the day. We were entertained by sheep and goats close up, and sailboats in the distance on the IJsselmeer. We were the only in-line skaters on the dike path, but there were plenty of bicyclists, mostly riding the upright cruisers so common in Holland. No Lycra-clad speedsters here, just folks out for a pleasant ride in the country. . . .

Reaching Medemblik, we took off our skates and set out for a quick tour of town and lunch. We watched as a fleet of boats passed under the raised drawbridge. The bridge keeper has a wooden shoe that he dangles from a string at the end of a pole, which is used to collect the toll from the passing helmsmen. There must be thousands of drawbridges in Holland!

—Excerpt from the travel diary of Dan Kibler, a Zephyr Tours Holland week participant, freelance skate photographer, and the author's at-home roll model

---

that new skates often take a while to break in, so get that out of the way before your scheduled tour.

If you plan to pack high-end racing skates, be sure to include your most comfy pair of fitness skates to give your feet the occasional break. Because skates designed for speed have a lot less padding and very little ankle support, touring for a few hours on these day after day can take its toll.

Taller wheels (76–80 mm) help you skate faster if you like to stay at the head of the pack or gain time for sightseeing at the day's destination. Because outdoor paving can vary in smoothness, it's best to choose wheels with a softer rating (76A as opposed to 80A or 82A) to better absorb road vibrations. You'll roll easier if your skates are outfitted with ABEC 5 bearings.

Essential Gear

____ skates

____ helmet and knee, elbow, and wrist guards

____ sunglasses

____ sunblock

____ water bottle or other drinking system

____ skate pack roomy enough to carry the day's necessities (listed below)

Skate Pack Contents

____ water (bottle or drinking system pack)

____ energy bar(s)

____ ID, medical insurance card, car keys, and a little cash

____ skate tool and spare parts

____ spare bearing, axle guide, nut and bolt sets, rockering spacer, and washer

____ light footwear if you're planning to enter business establishments

____ sweatshirt or windbreaker if weather indicates the need

Optional Items

____ spare heel brake for your skate model

____ heart rate monitor

____ skate-mounted computer and spare battery

____ first-aid kit

____ wrist guard–mounted rear view mirror

____ cell phone

____ skate carrier

Dan Kibler

Packing for a skate tour in the Netherlands.

Post-Skate Comforts

___ comb and cap for "helmet hair"

___ beverage and snack

___ large towel (for wiping salty skin or to stretch on)

___ dry socks and a warm, dry top for cold days

Packing for a Skate Tour Vacation

Besides the skates, skate pack, and items in the checklists above, bring along the following when heading off to join a multiday guided skate tour.

Clothes

___ two or three pairs of bike-style or loose-fitting shorts

___ two or three T-shirts, tank tops, or halter tops

___ two or three pairs of wicking athletic socks

___ rain-resistant windbreaker for wet or windy days

___ lightweight fleece top or sweatshirt for cool days

___ sandals or lightweight shoes you can easily carry while skating

___ several mix-and-matchable sets of casual wear for going out to dinner (jeans or khakis, polo or other low-wrinkle knit tops, a sweater)

___ walking shoes for evening activities

Touring and Traveling Aids

___ red flashing helmet light and front-mounted headlamp (might be required for attending a night skate)

___ appropriate adapter and converter for electric devices (blow dryer) if signing up for a European tour

___ camera and film

___ credit and ATM cards

___ local guidebook and maps

___ Swiss army knife with a corkscrew

___ wristwatch with an alarm or mini alarm clock

___ plastic bag to separate dirty laundry

___ small container of liquid laundry soap for hand-washing

TOURING RESOURCES

ORGANIZATIONS

Zephyr Inline Skate Tours, Inc.
This outfit guides skaters in areas selected for beautiful scenery, cultural richness, and smooth, flat pavement. Living up to its slogan, "Skate the World," Zephyr offers North American and overseas tours for beginner through expert skaters (888-758-8087, <www.skatetour.com>).

CITIES WITH NIGHT SKATES

Amsterdam, The Netherlands: <www.fridaynightskate.com>; home page of Amsterdam Friday Night Skate in the Netherlands. See also <www.te.nl> for Netherlands in-line skate tour guide booklets (in Dutch).

Berlin, Germany: <ourworld.compuserve.com/homepages/r_b/berlin.htm>; home page for Skating in Berlin, with information in German about group skates every first and third Wednesday.

Boston MA: <www.sk8net.com/events/nightskates/index.html>; information on night skates sponsored by InLine Club of Boston (ICB).

Frankfurt, Germany: <www.frankfurt-inline.de>; information on skating in and around Frankfurt.

Houston TX: <www.skatehouston.com/urban.html>; information on Houston's Urban Skaters and weekly skate routes.

London, England: <www.ucl.ac.uk/~uczxros/sk8whton.htm>; home page for London's regularly scheduled Monday, Wednesday, and summertime Friday Night Skates.

Los Angeles CA: <members.aol.com/theSWAN19/FridayNightSkate.htm>; information about the FNS through the streets of Santa Monica on the first and third Fridays of each month.

Minneapolis MN: <www.skatetour.com/friday.htm>; information about when and where to join the bimonthly FNS.

New York City NY: <www.skatecity.com/nyc/clubs/group.html>; descriptions of the Tuesday Night Skate, Empire Thursday Evening Roll, and Blade Night Manhattan on Wednesdays.

Paris, France: <www.pari-roller.com>; Pari-Roller Web site, home of the world's largest Friday Night Skate (the documented record was 28,000 in summer of 1999; verbal reports were up to 30,000). A professionally trained squad of in-line police officers accompanies the skaters. Text is in French.

Portland OR: <www.geocities.com/Colosseum/Stadium/5304/tuesdaynite.htmv>; details about the Tuesday Night Skate.

San Diego CA: <www.pilot.com/sdsc>; home page of the San Diego Skate Club, sponsoring a FNS.

San Francisco CA: <web.cora.org/friday.phtml>; home page for San Francisco's Midnight Rollers, the original Friday Night Skate.

Scottsdale AZ: <www.azinline.org/happngs.html#anchor18270>; details about the Wednesday Night Skate sponsored by the Arizona Inline Skating Club.

Seattle WA: <www.wilsa.org/moon>; home page of the Rollerwolves FNS.

PUBLICATIONS

1,000 Great Rail-Trails: A Comprehensive Directory. Greg Smith and Karen-Lee Ryan. Washington DC: Rails-to-Trails Conservancy, 1999.

California In-Line Skating: The Complete Guide to the Best Places to Skate. Liz Miller. Santa Rosa CA: Foghorn Press, 1996.

In-Line Skate New England: The Complete Guide to the Best 101 Tours. Cynthia Copeland Lewis, Thomas Lewis, and Carolyn Bradley. Woodstock VT: Countryman Press, 1997.

InLine Skating in Greater Boston. Boston: InLine Club of Boston Publishing, 1998.

(continued on next page)

TOURING RESOURCES *(continued from previous page)*

Rolling Around Puget Sound. David McCreary. Port Orchard WA: Pride & Imprints, 1998.

Skating Unrinked: An Insider's Guide to Skating Trails in the San Francisco Bay Area. Richard Katz. New York: HarperCollins, 1994.

Southern Ontario Inline Skating Guide. Mike Seca and Ron Seca. Toronto, Ontario: Stoddart Publishing Co., Limited, 1995.

The Ultimate Skating Guide to the San Francisco Bay Area. Todd Ray. Santa Rosa CA: Vision Books International, 1995.

CHAPTER FIVE

SKATE-TO-SKI

DIALECT

carving: Riding one or both sets of wheel edges around the curved arc of a turn; commonly used in describing slalom turns.

corresponding edges: The outside (right) edge of the right skate's wheels corresponds to the inside (right) edge of the left skate's wheels, and vice versa. When both skates are tipped in the same direction, they are on corresponding edges.

edging: The act of changing the angle of contact between the skate edges and the pavement.

fall line: On a hill, an imaginary line from the top to the bottom. This is the direction with the most gravitational pull.

parallel turns: A turn on corresponding edges.

"terminal velocity": The speed at which fear strips away an individual's known skills and crashing appears to be the only recourse.

It's your first day of skiing for the season. You've warmed up on some cruisers and now you're ready for the first challenging run of the year. Will you be able to summon the skills you had at the end of last season? What if you could ski that tough run *better* than you ever have before? That's more than possible for skiers who take up the in-line discipline known as skate-to-ski.

Winter's magical moments are a direct result of an improved ready position and better edging skills after a season of skate cross training. On a challenging ski run, the moment old habits tempt you to bend forward at the waist you will automatically resist, because that position moves your weight too far ahead of your ski boots. There are no ski tips or tails to lean on during your skate

Ski season is over, but not the carving!

training, which lets you make a habit of turning from a more upright position with your weight centered over your arches. Carving drills on skates can help you eliminate bad habits such as skidding around turns or pushing a stiff lower leg down the hill to "put on the brakes."

This chapter introduces downhill skating drills to develop a slalom technique that can dramatically improve your performance on alpine skis. The better your skills on wheels, the more fun you'll have this winter!

Gear

For a day of ski cross training, your regular helmet is fine. Pack a skate tool and fresh heel brake, just in case. For better protection in a long, sliding crash, wear long, heavy shorts and heavy-duty or sleeve-style knee and elbow pads that won't slip off your joints. Wrist guards work with ski pole grips that have a web strap. Otherwise, substitute a pair of heavy gardener's gloves or, at a minimum, bicycle gloves for abrasion protection.

If you have an old pair of ski poles, cover the tips by dipping them in rubber tool dip (available at hardware stores) or slip an old tennis ball over each end. If you're buying new poles just for skating, check out the mountaineering poles made by Leki that feature adjustable lengths and interior springs to absorb the jarring of ground contact. A cork grip adds to the comfort. You can set these to a longer length for Nordic-style cross-country skating or shorten them for downhill slaloms.

Hard-boot, four-wheel skates with a high cuff are best; they supply the necessary ankle support for skate-to-ski training. As in a ski boot, the rigid construction of such skates prevents excess lateral ankle movement and gives you more precise control of your feet. Four-wheel frames are much more maneuverable than five-wheelers. If you have a comfortable old pair of plastic recreation skates, they might be just the ticket!

For better turn carving, purchase a set of Parabolics in-line wheels, which are the asphalt version of the shaped ski revolution. These are specially designed to add an inherent arc to each carved turn because a fat third wheel becomes a pivot point that results in a tighter radius. Until now, the problem of carving tight turns has been a drawback in skate-to-ski.

Key Skills

To practice the following drills safely, you should have excellent braking and speed control skills as described in chapter 2.

Slalom Posture

The techniques of edging, turning, and speed control require an athletic, upright crouch. A proper ready position is easy to lose under the duress of skating downhill at high speeds or when trying to master the technical aspects of ski technique, yet it is a required fundamental across the board.

The skiing-ready position is an athletic crouch with the following qualities.

Dan Kibler

Parabolic wheels.

- **Alignment:** With eyes and head up and chest facing forward (not down), bounce gently up and down to find a structurally aligned stance with your shoulders over your hips and hips over ankles and with all three sets of joints comfortably flexed.

- **Spine:** First, arch your spine into a tight swayback position. Feel how stiff your upper body has become. A tight or arched lower back is the first sign of tenseness; it compromises your flexibility and balance. Now curve your spine in the opposite direction, rounding your pelvis and shoulders forward. Stretch your back this way for a second and then relax with your hips tucked slightly forward, directly under your shoulders. This rounded back is the natural skeleton-supporting posture you're looking for.

- **Shoulders:** With hands and bent elbows at the same height, squeeze your shoulder blades together tightly. Now separate the shoulder blades as far as possible and watch how far your hands extend ahead of you without changing the way you are holding your arms.

- **Hand position:** Your hands must always be visible! Even without poles, hold your hands away from your body, slightly to the sides where you can see them. With one or both hands behind you, expect a backward loss of balance. For tight turns, the hands always follow a straight downhill path, with the shoulders facing the bottom of the hill. For giant slalom (long) turns, the hands and upper body face the tangent of the turn instead of the bottom of the hill.

Your rounded spine and shoulders, elbows, and hands should be shaped like a pair of crossed Cs. This is the ideal position for seriously fun (and in-control) downhill slaloms.

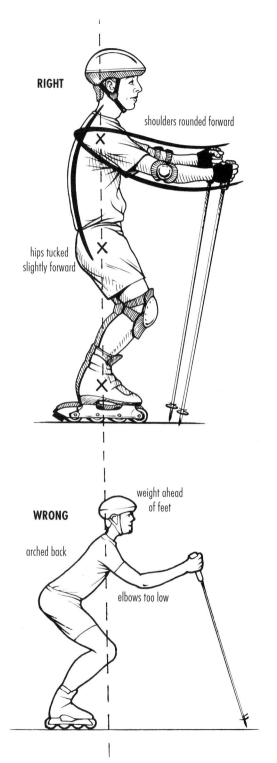

Proper slalom stance.

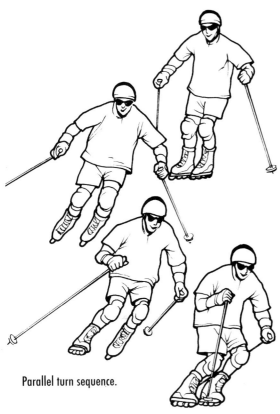

Parallel turn sequence.

Basic Technique

Slalom turns are best learned on a gentle grade with a long, flat runout. Going faster than your comfort level will cause you to shift your weight too far back for good speed control, which results in terminal velocity! Lacking a slope, stroke hard to build up speed to perform the drills or skate with a strong tailwind if one's available.

Learn how to carve effective slalom turns *before* introducing the added complication of ski poles. Basic turns are based on the intermediate skater's slalom or "serpentine" skill.

1. Start rolling down your practice hill in an upright ready position with hips, knees, and ankles well flexed.

2. Move your left skate, hip, and shoulder slightly forward; then edge and steer both skates to the left, applying pressure to the right skate's inside edges.

3. To change direction, allow your mid-section to rise up and cross over your skates. By edging and steering your skates toward the bottom of the hill while maintaining a stable upper body, you will again find a position in which your inside (right)skate, hip, and shoulder are slightly ahead. This is called *lead change*.

4. After a few practice runs, start making smaller-radius turns. Keep your shoulders facing downhill as your legs work from right to left under you.

5. Enter each turn by rising slightly to allow the weight shift; finish it by flexing your hips and knees toward the inside of the turn, applying pressure to the carving skate.

6. Practice until you can complete a series of rhythmic, linked slaloms.

Progress to a more dynamic slalom turn.

1. Begin to sink into each turn by flexing your hips and knees toward the inside of the turn and increasing the tilt of your edges. The resulting increased pressure on both uphill edges is what aids in speed control.

2. To initiate the next turn, release the pressure on the skates by allowing your midsection to move up and over your skates, ending up on the new set of edges. This results in a moment of lightness known as unweighting.

3. Allow the edging skates to generate tighter slalom turns. Listen for the audible sound of successful carving: urethane literally being scrubbed from the sides of your wheels!

Skate-to-Ski Training

Practice the following techniques on a slope steep enough to roll at a moderate pace without stroking but gentle enough for easy midrun speed reduction or stopping to avoid sudden danger (see Hill Skills on page 28). Build your slalom skills without ski poles at first.

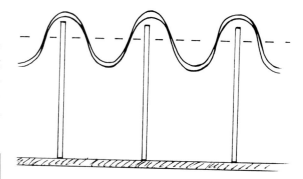

Slaloming the ends of parking space lines.

PRACTICE TIP

These may be skate drills, but they work just as well on skis!

Relax and Angulate

When you loosen up your midsection, it's easier to keep your upper body quiet and centered as your lower body sweeps from turn to turn.

Find an empty, sloped parking lot that will allow you to slalom the ends of the painted parking space lines. This drill is ideal for skiers who want to improve their flexibility and speed for mogul runs.

1. Start rolling downhill toward the end of the first parking space line.

2. Slalom around the end of the first line and then steer both skates toward the middle of the second line. As you cross it, steer both skates back toward the end of the third line and try to skate around it, missing the paint.

3. Relax your torso. Use only enough abdominal strength to keep your upper body vertical as you allow your skates to swing and extend as far to the side as possible. Your head should travel a straight line down the middle.

Carve Skid-Free Turns

One-footed carves on skates are one of the best ski cross training exercises, because they force the

body to stay centered over the carving edge and reduce the tendency to shove the tail of the (nonexistent) "ski" downhill and skid. When you're turning at high speeds, a skid can cause a crash.

Speed picks up if you let your skates roll in tandem during the transitions between slaloms. The sooner you shift your weight onto the new turning skate, the better it can begin edging to cut speed, and the less likely you are to skid.

ALTERNATING ONE-FOOT SLALOMS

Practice this often to improve your carving precision, speed control, and turn timing. Do not try to keep your shoulders facing downhill.

1. Start rolling down your practice hill.

2. The moment you complete the weight shift to initiate a turn, raise the inactive skate an inch or so off the pavement.

3. Sink into the turn, riding on just the one skate until it crosses the fall line.

4. As you cross over into the new turn, swap your weight to the new outside skate as you lift the other off the pavement. The weight shift should feel similar to pedaling a bicycle half a crank. Skiers, this pedaling foot swap is also the moment of pole plant.

5. Sink hip-over-heel into your next turn.

6. Carve large turns all the way down your

hill, never allowing both skates to be in contact with the pavement at the same time.

7. At the bottom of your hill, make the turnaround to skate back up by riding out a one-footed carve on your weakest leg. Do this often enough, and you'll no longer have a weak leg!

LATERAL HOP TURNS

This drill generates skiing and skating confidence while improving turn timing. It's very important that you keep your hands forward and your knees well bent.

1. Start slaloming down your practice hill, keeping your upper body facing down the fall line in a well-flexed ready position.

2. At the moment your wheels reach maximum pressure on the pavement, make a low hop toward the center of the new turn.

One-foot slaloms.

3. In that brief midair moment, shift both feet laterally across the fall line while your skates rotate slightly toward the new turn direction. Meanwhile, keep your shoulders facing squarely down the fall line.

4. Land with your legs extended and then gradually sink into the turn. Continue hopping to initiate each turn, concentrating on a narrow stance as your feet shift from side to side with each hop. Start out so smooth that an observer would hardly notice your skates have left the pavement. Work up to more energetic hops and a greater sideways midair shift of the skates.

When using ski poles, time the pole plant with the beginning of the hop.

SLALOM A COURSE

Set up a row of cones in a straight line down the center of a slope. Skate down at varying speeds and work on timing your turns to cut as close as possible to the "gates." For a more challenging course, vary the distances and alignment of the cones.

Improve Balance and Agility

Once you've conquered alternating one-foot slaloms, it's time to move on to linked slalom turns on the same foot. This ability improves your balance tremendously and pays dividends in all carving abilities, including slipping through a mogul field.

SAME-FOOT SLALOMS

Start out on the flats by building up speed and then coasting into a series of quick, tiny slalom turns to get a rhythm going. After completing three or four carves, lift one foot off the pavement and continue the quick rhythm by slaloming on the other skate.

When doing one-foot slaloms, allow your upper body to move freely and naturally. Enforcing a rigid stance will inhibit your ability to balance over and work the edges of your skate. Once this becomes too easy, try slaloming on one foot through a row of cones.

ROLL MODEL

Over the years, I have helped hundreds of young ski racers train in the summer months using in-line skates. The results I have seen from these skiers have converted me to a firm believer in skate-to-ski.

The benefits of in-line skating for skiers are not limited to simple simulation of skiing but are as open ended as the field of in-line skating itself. Perhaps the greatest gift I have seen bestowed upon the skate-to-ski practitioner is the overall skill development offered through the use of in-lines. Like skiing, in-line skating is a gliding sport. The refinement of general athletic ability, balance, spatial orientation, and more go a long way to creating a better overall skier and can make a significant difference when the snow arrives. So when you are done with your sport-specific drills, get out and have a blast on your skates. Skate backward, spin, swizzle, lunge, slide, and jump your way to better turns once you get on the boards.

—Adam Steer, Director of IISA Canada and Skate-to-Ski Certification Program examiner; certified alpine ski instructor and coach

Skate with Ski Poles

Slalom skating without a pair of ski poles translates beautifully to ski technique. However, using poles for your dry-land cross training is an excellent way to improve timing and develop a posture that enhances rather than hinders your skiing form. Drilling with poles can help you learn when to initiate and complete your turns, maintain proper arm placement, and improve your balance over the ski's "sweet spot." A pair of poles also makes steeper hills seem less scary.

To learn how to skate with ski poles, set up some mini cones or other small, weighted objects about 15 feet apart in a line down a gentle hill.

1. Start rolling from the top and slalom around the first cone.

2. At the end of a turn to the right, most of your weight is over the left skate. Extend your left arm and wrist to firmly plant the pole tip to the pavement directly ahead to initiate a new turn to the left.

3. At the same time, allow your midsection to cross over your skates as you shift your weight to the right skate to start turning toward the left.

4. Keep that left hand in front of your body as you carve to the left around the sta-

tionary pole tip. Keep the grip moving forward with your line of travel.

5. To begin turning right, plant your right pole. At the same time, cross over your skates and steer them into the carve as you shift your weight to the new outside (left) skate.

6. Begin each turn with a pole plant well before you reach the cone you are turning

Dan Kibler

Ski cross training with poles.

around. Since you are halfway around the turn by the time you pass the cone, both skates should be pointing straight down the hill as you pass beside it.

7. Vary your speed and the size of your turns. Work on keeping both hands in front of your body where you can see them. If necessary, drill on this by forcefully punching your fist down the fall line at the moment the pole tip touches the pavement.

When using poles for alpine ski cross training, remember these tips.

- Grip the poles firmly but don't squeeze.

- Keep your elbows raised to hand level so that your arms are rounded, not bent.

- Your hands should always be in view. Avoid dropping your planting hand and rotating around the pole plant.

- Use the ski pole to mark your rhythm. Plant it on the pavement as you cross over into the next turn.

- Flick the pole tip forward by swiveling your wrist rather than jabbing from a bent elbow. This is easy when you remain upright with elbows at hand height. Quick flicks can help you make faster, tighter turns.

- For better speed and edge control on steep hills, plant the pole as far down the line of travel as possible while retaining the proper stance.

- Keep your chest facing forward, not down. If you bend at the waist you will have trouble controlling your speed and keeping your poles high enough to plant without jabbing.

 SKATE-TO-SKI RESOURCES

CAMPS

In Quebec, Michel Pratte's Race 'n Roll camps feature morning coaching clinics on slalom technique followed by a variety of outdoor activities including fitness training, volleyball, and rock climbing (USA 800-641-3327 and fax 800-641-3324, Canada 800-265-7580 and fax 800-641-3324, <www.mprattesport.com/english/camps/camps.htm>).

Skate-to-Ski Camps conducted by Debbie Sumner, Level 2 Certified Instructor; multiday camp emphasizes the benefits of in-line skating for staying in shape and cross training for alpine skiing. Beginner, intermediate, and advanced skaters participate in daily training clinics, skating gates, touring, and more (877-SK8-CALI/877-758-2254, fax 714-964-4799, e-mail: dasasports@aol.com).

WEBSITES

<www.getrolling.com/orbitIndex.html> Lists links to downhill articles in the Get Rolling Orbit, an online skater's newsletter.

<www.members.aol.com/wwskiclub/inline.htm> Westwood Ski and Sports Club lists skate-to-ski training and competition schedules and is downhill expert Scott Peer's home base.

WHEELS

Parabolics Sports Systems, Inc.
100 Alexis Nihon Blvd.,
   Suite 909
St. Laurent PQ
Canada H4M 2P4
888-430-7979 or
   514-855-9000
fax 514-855-1444
E-mail: skatebetter@parabolics.com
www.parabolics.com/home.html
Parabolics in-line wheels for tighter turns on skates.

CHAPTER SIX

FREESTYLE

DIALECT (STREET DANCING)

cross back (left or right): Passing one skate in back of the other and stepping onto it with the toe just behind the support skate.

cross front (left or right): Passing one skate in front of the other and stepping onto it with the heel angled toward the support skate.

heel up (left or right): Raising one skate's toe and pushing its heel slightly ahead of the support skate's toe (*up* in this context means advanced, not raised).

one-foot turn: Pivoting on one skate to complete a quarter-, half-, or full turn.

one-two: Lifting each skate up and down in turn as though marching in place; typically used to end a combination.

step in between: A neutralizing step in which the skates are returned to a shoulder-width stance with all wheels on the ground; used to keep time and transition between other movements.

In-line skating draws us because of the sheer joy that comes from stroking and gliding, a feeling that is as close as humans ever get to unfettered flight. Freestyle skating, with its precise but seemingly effortless moves, liberates the human soul in an even more transcendent way. Whether it's Rollerdance, figure skating, or snaking artistically down a slalom course, freestyle offers its participants a chance to abandon themselves to the joy of physical expression while developing incredible balance, coordination, and body awareness. Unfortunately, (in my opinion) they also tend to abandon protective gear as well, as you'll notice in this chapter's photos.

This chapter describes three forms of freestyle skating that most in-liners enjoy for fun and exercise: figure (artistic) skating, street-style roller or disco dancing, and slaloming in creative ways through a field of cones. In areas with enough people and interest, these activities also make great opportunities for competition.

STREET DANCING

Street dancing can be an excellent nonimpact aerobic workout. Skaters who dance enjoy a level of athletic artistic expression comparable to what made Jazzercize so popular in the 1980s. It's a great way to make new friends, but it's just as fun to do solo. Dancing on skates makes you more balanced and agile, making it complementary to your other in-line interests no matter what they are.

In large metropolitan areas, notably San Francisco, Chicago, Venice Beach in California, and New York City, in-line dancers meet at the local hot spots to express themselves to music. Because musical preference, choreography, and step names vary by location and continue to evolve over time, it can be difficult for novices who don't live in the area to get started. In San Francisco, however, an enterprising dance instructor named Richard Humphrey assembled a breakdown of several core steps to produce videos for his Rollerdance program. His standard set of movements allows skaters of all levels to learn to dance on in-lines or conventional quad skates.

In the United States, formal skate dancing competitions emerged in the late 1990s with the Red Bull Great Skate series, sponsored by Red Bull energy drink and produced by Makai Events. A full season of local competitions culminates in the National Finals each year. Amateur and professional dancers five years and older compete to their own choice of music on a 40' × 40' stage. Female and male soloists, pairs, and teams of three to eight skaters are judged on their talent, skill, and creativity. Costumes are optional, but coordinated outfits are common.

There is no organizing body for street dancing to date.

Gear

Dance on the type of skates that makes you most comfortable: both short frame in-lines and roller (quad) skates work fine. Don't forget to wear pads and a helmet.

Tips for Success

- Take a lesson or hang out with the local dancers in your area.
- Warm up before each session for better flexibility and less strain on muscles and joints.
- Be sure to drink enough water to stay hydrated during your dance (exercise!) sessions.
- Start by learning the simplest steps; then progress to more complex combinations as you gain agility.
- Try new steps in stocking feet first to get a better muscular and mental image of the movement.
- Remove your heel brake for dance sessions so it won't get in the way, trip you during cross steps, or scuff indoor flooring.
- Choose lively music that inspires you to dance.
- Keep your knees loose and bent between steps.
- Practice being smooth and fluid; try not to make clomping noises when setting down your skates.
- Keep the tempo slow when learning new steps. Dance in half-time to your music or leave it turned off.
- When not dancing, work on one-footed balance to make the more advanced steps easier to learn.

Dan Kibler

Dancing in synchronicity.

ROLL MODEL

Richard Humphrey dreamed of sharing his love of street dancing for years before finally producing his first *Rollerdancing* video. After skating virtually nonstop since the mid-1970s, he produced his video to help skaters who are eager to take their first steps in the art of roller dancing. Richard demonstrates on video the steps he has been teaching for the last two decades. Although printed documentation is rare with this discipline, he also provides a fully illustrated guide to all the steps and movements.

Humphrey continues to spread his love of Rollerdancing doing demonstrations and seminars and making television and charity appearances all over the world. Today there are three videos in the Rollerdance collection. (See Freestyle Resources at the end of this chapter.)

—Richard Humphrey, northern California Rollerdance instructor, choreographer, video producer, and international performer

Sample Rollerdance Steps

The following two moves offer just a taste of West Coast Rollerdance, so you can start learning this form of street dancing in the privacy of your own home. Once you can do them gracefully in time to a lively beat, you'll be ready to learn more advanced combinations or to get out in public and join a local dance group.

Regular

This Rollerdance step is a combination of basic moves defined by name in the Dialect sidebar, page 73. It consists of a series of steps toward the right and is then repeated toward the left.

1. **Right heel up:** Starting from a ready position, push your right skate ahead and slightly to the right side so the toe is up and only the heel wheel is in contact with the ground. You have assumed the starting position for most Rollerdance steps.

2. **Step in between:** Lift the right skate and step to the right, setting the right skate down directly beneath the hip.

3. **Cross front:** Pass the left skate in front of the right and return all four wheels to the ground, slightly to the right of the right skate.

4. **Step in between:** Bring the right skate out from behind the left and step to the right, returning the skate to the ground directly beneath the hip.

5. **Cross back:** Pass the left skate in back and slightly beyond the right skate and step onto it.

6. **One-two:** Slightly lift first the right skate and then the left to reposition yourself in a neutral, shoulder-width ready position.

7. Repeat all the moves in the opposite direction, starting with left heel up, and continue moving back and forth until the movement becomes fluid.

Long

Note that the first five movements of Long are exactly the same as in Regular. The last two steps plus repetition are what make it "long."

1. **Right heel up:** Starting from a ready position, push the right skate ahead and slightly to the right side so the toe is up and only the heel wheel is in contact with the ground.

2. **Step in between:** Step to the right and set the right skate down directly beneath the hip.

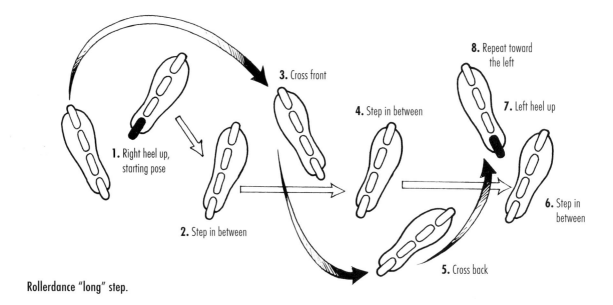

Rollerdance "long" step.

3. **Cross front:** Pass the left skate in front of and slightly beyond the right and return all four wheels to the ground.

4. **Step in between:** Bring the right skate out from behind the left and step to the right, returning the skate to the ground directly beneath the hip.

5. **Cross back:** Pass the left skate in back and slightly beyond the right skate and step onto it.

6. **Step in between:** Step to the right and set the right skate down directly beneath the hip.

7. **Left heel up:** Push the left skate ahead and slightly to the side so the toe is up and only the heel wheel is in contact with the ground.

8. Repeat all the moves in the opposite direction and continue moving back and forth until the movement becomes fluid.

ARTISTIC SKATING

As a member of Team Rollerblade in the early days, figure skater Jill Schulz attracted America's attention with a deftly executed repertoire of jumps and spins. Graceful as she was on her classic TRS Lightening skates, in-line technology at that time left much to be desired for ice and roller skaters who wanted to duplicate their favorite moves outdoors or on pavement.

Our famous American ingenuity stepped up to the task. In 1997, Harmony Sports introduced the PIC frame, a rockered aluminum wheel frame with a rink-safe, urethane toe unit that can be used exactly like an ice skate's toe pick. Today, the PIC Skate Company sells this frame alone or mounted on a wide choice of quality leather boots, complete with padded lining and tongue and steel shank arches. With this setup, figure skaters can perform virtually every maneuver, including spirals, spread eagles, camel spins, bauers, lutz jumps, 3-turns, sal-chows, and choctaws.

The national governing body for artistic skating is USA Roller Skating (USA/RS), recognized as such by the United States Olympic Committee. Skaters interested in performing in competitions must be registered with USA/RS. Members of USA/RS-chartered clubs can participate in local, regional, and national competitions. Membership also includes supplementary medical and dental insurance.

DIALECT (ARTISTIC SKATING)

EDGES

center edge: The place on the wheels that is in contact with the pavement when the skate is perpendicular to the surface.

inside edge: The sides of the wheels below the foot's arch.

LFI edge: Indicates forward movement while rolling on the left skate's inside edge.

LFO edge: Indicates forward movement while rolling on the left skate's outside edge.

outside edge: The sides of the wheels below the outside edge of the foot.

RFI edge: Indicates forward movement while rolling on the right skate's inside edge.

RFO edge: Indicates forward movement while rolling on the right skate's outside edge.

SPINS

barrel roll: A spin launched and landed on the heel wheels, performed in a seated position with the skater's arms rounded in front and held parallel to the ground and the thighs.

camel spin: A spin performed on one skate in spiral position; that is, with the body and free leg held horizontal to the ground or, when flexibility allows, with the free leg elevated above the head.

sit spin: A spin performed with the skater squatting low over the heel of the support leg while the free leg is extended straight ahead just above and parallel to the ground ("shoot-the-duck position").

JUMPS

axel: An airborne revolution launched from the outside edge of a forward-gliding skate and landed on the outside edge of the nonlaunching skate's wheels, either forward or backward. There are half, single, double, and triple axels.

euler: An airborne revolution launched from the outside edge of a backward-gliding skate and landed in a backward glide on the inside edges of the nonlaunching skate's wheels. Also known as a *half loop*.

flip: A full-revolution backward flip launched from the inside edge of a backward-gliding skate and the pick of the opposite skate and landed in a backward glide on the outside edge of the skate that picked.

loop: A full airborne revolution launched from the outside edge of a backward-gliding skate and landed in a backward glide on that same skate's outside wheel edges. This is more difficult than the flip, because it is launched from an outside edge.

lutz: A backward flip launched from the outside edge of a backward-gliding skate and the pick of the opposite skate and landed in a backward glide on the outside edge of the skate that picked.

salchow: A jump launched from the inside edge of a backward-gliding skate and landed in a backward glide on the outside edge of the nonlaunching skate's wheels.

toe loop (also known as a *Mapes jump*): A jump launched from the outside edge of a backward-gliding skate and the pick of the opposite skate and landed in a backward glide on the outside edge of the skate that did not pick.

waltz: A half-revolution jump launched from the outside edge of a forward-gliding skate and landed on in a backward glide on the outside edge of the other skate.

Before launching a figure skating specialty, you should already be comfortable turning on both inside edges (A-frame turns, spin stops, and swizzles) and outside edges (parallel turns, slaloms). It also helps to be adept at skating and turning backward (including backward crossovers) and performing coordinated maneuvers such as heel-toe rolls (see page 33).

Gear

With the introduction of PIC Skates and others like them, figure skaters are able to enjoy artistic skating wherever there's a clean surface, both indoors and outdoors, without the need for ice.

Other skate manufacturers, such as Atlas, Snyder Skate Company, and the SP Teri Company, offer skates with similar frames.

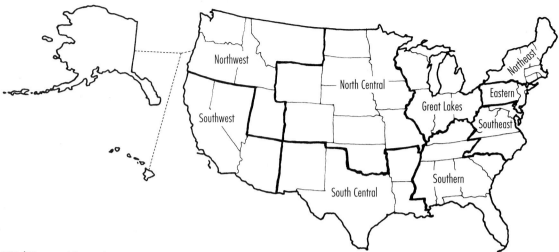

USA/RS competition regions.

What you choose for artistic skating depends on personal preference, past experience, where you'll be skating, and the available technology. For the most part, roller rink–oriented skaters use traditional "quad" roller skates, although some, along with ice figure skaters, have begun wearing PIC Skates on rink floors. Outdoors, artistic skaters can choose quad skates, recreational four-wheel in-line skates, or PIC Skates. These are usually outfitted with softer wheels to improve grip on a rougher surface.

Don't leave your protective gear behind. At a minimum, wear a helmet and wrist guards during indoor and outdoor practice sessions. Knee and elbow pads are especially important when learning new moves.

PIC Skates sighting in Golden Gate Park.

Getting Started

Harmony Sports's Gym Skate Program introduces youngsters to fundamental artistic skating basics in a gym setting as part of a school's physical education curriculum. See the Freestyle Resources section at the end of this chapter for more information about this program.

But you don't have to be a kid to take up and compete in figure skating. The USA/RS age divisions are from 6 to 60, and beginners' divisions are included at all regional, national, and world competitions.

Sample Artistic Moves

Spiral (also known as an arabesque)

The Spiral is an elegant move that intermediate-level skaters with good one-footed balance can easily begin to learn. Flexible folks earn style points based on how high above the head they can get the raised skate to achieve the classic "champagne glass" pose. Be sure to warm up and stretch, including a couple of stationary practice poses while holding onto a stable support, before attempting this move.

1. Push with the right skate so you are coasting forward on the left foot with the

ROLL MODEL

Everyone who in-line skates should consider jumping and spinning! It is so much fun. You don't have to be an advanced figure skater; on in-lines, there really are no rules, so you can even create your own moves. Just imagine how impressed your friends will be when they see you perform a small jump, glide into a spiral, or start spinning on one foot. They'll want to try it too.

For me, jumping and spinning on in-lines always reminds me of why I enjoy skating. It is so challenging, and there's always something new to try—I am never bored! Learning to jump and spin adds another satisfying dimension to in-line skating; but remember, the main thing is to simply go out there and have fun!

—Jo Ann Schneider Farris, instructor and author of *How to Jump and Spin on In-Line Skates*

left knee slightly bent. With both arms stretched out to the sides and your torso erect, extend the right foot behind you.

2. Raise the free skate until the leg is parallel with the ground (or higher) and straighten the knee of the support leg.

3. Rotate the raised leg outward at the hip and extend the foot so your toe is turned out and pointed.

4. To assume the classic pose, lean forward as you continue lifting the leg beyond 90 degrees. Make sure your center of gravity is centered solidly over the support leg.

5. To exit the spiral, raise your torso and then lower the leg.

Once a straight-ahead spiral seems easy, practice tracing a curved path by utilizing either the support skate's inside or outside edge. You can also learn to perform spirals while gliding backward.

Shoot the Duck

This move requires flexibility and strength as well as balance and coordination. It's easier if there's no heel brake on the skate you extend out in front.

1. Starting from a fast, forward two-foot glide, drop into a deep squat (a dip) with your hips riding just behind your heels.

2. With your left hand on your right knee, grip your right calf with the right hand

Shoot the duck.

and lift the right skate forward and ahead until the leg is straight.

3. Coast as far as your balance and speed allow.

4. To get up, return the right skate next to the left and then rise on both feet from the dip.

5. As you get better, start lifting the right skate at the same time you begin dropping your hips so that the skate is fully extended and off the ground by the time you reach a full dip. Skaters with strong legs and good knee joints are able to rise by reversing this, without using hands or assuming a two-legged squat first.

3-Turn

Performed correctly, the 3-turn deftly transitions a skater gliding on one foot from forward to backward skating. It gets its name from the path it traces: The middle point of the 3 results from pivoting on one wheel. You'll need good one-footed balance, and if you can perform the toe or heel pivots described in the Directional Transitions section of chapter 9 (page 116), you've got a head start. This is simply a one-footed version.

You can do 3-turns on the left or right skate and on the inside or outside wheel edges. Most right-handed people find it easiest to learn a forward, clockwise 3-turn on the left foot's outside edges (an LFO 3-turn).

1. Hold your right arm in front of your body and your left arm in back. Spot a marker a few yards ahead throughout the move for better balance.

2. In an upright ready position, push off into a forward coast on the left foot (knee is bent) with the right skate held slightly behind the support leg.

3. Tip the left skate onto its outside wheel edges to start a shallow turn to the left.

4. As the left skate begins a curve, settle

your weight over its front half and begin rotating your hips toward the left.

5. In one quick movement, swing the free (right) skate forward and, pivoting briefly on the left skate's front toe wheel, rotate your heel and hips counterclockwise.

6. Return the left heel to the ground and finish the turn with a backward one-footed glide on the left skate's inside wheel edges.

7. Now that your upper body is facing backward to the direction of travel, your right arm is the back arm and your left arm is the front arm: You have rotated between your arms without changing their positions.

Once 3-turns become easy, practice them at higher speeds with a deeper preparatory arc on the support skate's outside edge. And of course, begin working on your LFI, RFO, and RFI 3-turns! The pivot is the same, but the approach and direction of the turn differ. When you're ready, dare to try backward 3-turns.

Two-Foot Spin

Catering once again to right-handers, here's how to achieve a counterclockwise spin over the left toe wheel and right heel wheel. A good practice exercise before you start is the heel-toe roll described on page 33.

1. Standing still with feet shoulder width apart, wind up for the spin by swinging both arms to the right, opposite the direction of the spin. It's okay if your upper body twists slightly to the right, but keep both skates planted firmly where they are.

2. Swing both arms abruptly across your body to the left, being careful to remain perfectly upright with your weight centered equally over both feet.

3. As your skates begin twisting counter-

clockwise in response to the arm swing, raise the left skate's heel and the right skate's toe an inch or so off the pavement.

4. Spinning on the right heel and left toe wheels, clasp both arms against your chest to accelerate the spin.

5. To exit a successful spin, drop your arms to slow down and return the raised wheels to the ground.

Competition

Beginning artistic roller skaters start with the USA/RS Junior Olympic Artistic Program, where they can hone their skills through practice, lessons, and competition. Eventually, they progress toward senior Olympic level USA/RS-sponsored competitions. Nine regional championships identify winners who compete in the annual United States Championships for national titles. From here, the top three male and female placers represent the United States at the annual World Artistic Championships.

Contestants are judged on their precision and artistry while competing in any of four disciplines: figures, singles, pairs, and dance. Competitive placement depends on the skills demonstrated and, excluding figures, how the skater or pair interprets and executes identifiable moves in a routine set to music.

As of this writing, in-line figure skaters remain a minority in contests and in some cases are required to compete in the same USA/RS events as quad skaters. Harmony Sports hosts independent in-line figure skating competitions to promote their PIC Skate.

- **Figures:** Contestants trace a series of patterns painted on the skating surface. Precision footwork wins: Those who can maintain balance and control while doing figures from a variety of demanding takeoffs, edges, and turns achieve award-winning accuracy.

- **Singles:** A choreographed singles performance includes jumps, spins, and footwork accompanied by music. Besides poise, showmanship, and confident footwork in transitional segments, winning performers demonstrate the greatest speed, height in jumps, control, velocity, and variety of spin positions.

- **Pairs:** Couples perform a synchronized routine where both partners attempt to match the other's movements. In addition to overhead lifts, pairs demonstrate simultaneous spins, jumps, and footwork in an athletic yet artistic program.

- **Dance:** Artistic dance is not to be confused with street-style dancing. There are three types of artistic dance competitions: compulsory dance, requiring specified patterns and musical rhythms; free dance, where teams do their best to interpret their selected music with original choreography and intricate footwork; and solo dance, where men and women compete in the same field.

SLALOMS WITH CONES

Slaloming through a series of cones, either on a level course or down a slope, is a fascinating form of freestyle found in such cities as Boston, Miami, Paris, New York, Chicago, and Santa Monica. While a ski-style parallel turn is a great way to start a slalom career, the true experts use a wide variety of body positions and turning techniques to snake their way to the bottom of a straight course of evenly spaced cones without knocking over any of them.

Gear

Roller (quad) skates or recreational in-lines work equally well for slalom courses. A shorter in-line frame is better for maneuverability than the longer frames used for fitness or speed skating. Wear your pads and helmet, urges the Safety Lady yet again.

DIALECT (SLALOMS WITH CONES)

alternating tricks: A run that alternates between two slalom methods that are swapped every few cones.

ballistics: Any high-speed slalom variation, made possible by a fast or descending approach.

combinations: Any mix of multiple slalom methods repeated in sequence down the course.

conehead: A devotee of cone-style slalom skating.

cones: Objects used to mark a slalom course. Cups are used in Paris. (Avoid using empty soft drink cans; when the can is crushed in a crash, the sharp aluminum edges can cut the skater quite severely.)

extended tricks: Variations with one skate (usually the leading skate) tilted so that only the heel wheel is touching the ground.

heel-and-toe: Forward, backward, or

sideways variations performed with one heel wheel and one toe wheel off the pavement.

one-toe-down: Any slalom method performed with either skate's heel raised off the pavement; also known as *tilted-skate tricks*.

pairs: Two people skating the course in tandem while holding hands.

toe-and-toe: Slaloms performed while balancing on both toe wheels.

Dan Kibler

Cone skaters often inspire awe.

The Course

A typical sloped slalom course in New York City is a series of 27 cones spaced 6 feet apart. Flat courses are often set up in a tighter formation, with the cones at least a foot closer together. "Technical courses" might be only about 15 cones long and are set up with the cones spaced from 2 to 4 feet apart. These are used in competition by advanced slalom skaters (described in chapter 10).

The length of the approach depends on the characteristics of the location and traffic flow. The length of the runout can be as little as 5 or 10 feet if the course is flat or up to 200 feet, depending on the pitch.

Sample Slalom Methods

The following descriptions of common slalom methods include the easiest technique (parallels) and a few not-so-easy variations for true conehead "wannabes."

Parallel Slalom

This most basic method is nothing more than linked slalom turns (see skate-to-ski Basic Technique on page 68). Scissors the uphill skate an inch ahead to initiate each turn and alternate shallow turns to trace a serpentine path around the cones. Use a narrow stance with your knees bent and your hands ahead and in view.

The backward parallel slalom is a more advanced version of the same movement.

Monoline

True to its name, the monoline traces a single, serpentine path through the cones, with one skate remaining in the lead for the entire run and both toes pointing downhill. To make the turns, tip both skates onto corresponding edges, alternating from left to right until the course is cleared. The backward version is performed the same way, but with both heels pointing down the hill.

One-Foot

Skaters slalom the cones either forward or backward on one skate only, with the inactive leg held off the pavement in any position. The upraised limb can be used for added turning torque or carried creatively to gain style points.

Side Surfing (a.k.a. "Sidewind")

To side surf, the trailing skate traces the same path as the front skate in a heel-to-heel, toes-out stance. This method is easiest for people with loose hip joints (or younger skaters who start stretching into the position early).

1. Rolling forward, transfer your weight briefly to the right skate.

2. Pivot the left skate 180 degrees to get into a heel-to-heel stance with both skates tracing the same line. This might be easier if you separate the skates by a foot or two and bend your knees 90 degrees.

3. Land the left skate on its outside edge, equalize your weight over both skates; then lean your upper body slightly backward, keeping your knees over your toes so the skates remain on center edges.

Forward heel-and-toe.

4. Pressure on both inside edges causes a turn toward the front side; pressure on both outside edges causes a turn toward the back side.

Criss-Cross

This forward or backward method alternates a standard swizzle movement with crossed thighs (it doesn't matter which thigh is in front). The skater alternates between passing over a cone with an open straddle on inside edges to passing over it in a crossed-thigh stance with skates tipped on the outside wheel edges.

FREESTYLE RESOURCES

ORGANIZATIONS AND MANUFACTURERS

Harmony Sports
(The PIC Skate Company)
P.O. Box 219
Malden MA 02148
Gym Skate Program:
    781-324-2272
PIC frame or PIC Skates:
    800-882-3448
E-mail: sales@picskate.com
www.picskate.com
Patent owner of the PIC Skate, Harmony Sports offers its Gym Skate Program to provide instruction to students in grades K-12. Equipped with a rental fleet of PIC Skates (nondamaging to gym floors), instructors teach basic skating skills in a gym setting.

USA Roller Skating
P.O. Box 6579
4730 South Street
Lincoln NE 68506
402-483-7551
fax 402-483-1465
E-mail: usacrs@usacrs.com
www.usacrs.com
Domestic governing body promoting roller sports via training, team support, and sanctioned hockey, artistic, and speed skatingcompetitions.

PUBLICATIONS

How to Jump and Spin on In-Line Skates. Jo Ann Schneider Farris. Colorado Springs: self-published, 1999 (719-632-4098).

VIDEOS

Rollerdance Workout (1997) and *Rollerdance Workout Parts 2 and 3* (1999). Richard Humphrey. San Francisco: Movement in Motion Productions (415-469-0909).

WEBSITES

<www.cpdsa.org> The Central Park Dance Skaters Association website directs dancers to events, a mailing list service, and five years of archived online newsletters (212-760-4848, e-mail: gene@cpdsa.org).

<www.skatecity.com/c+w/> The Cones and Wheels slalom site is no longer actively maintained but still full of useful information.

▪ PART TWO ▪

A COMPETITIVE START

CHAPTER SEVEN

SPEED SKATING

DIALECT

breakaway: A surprise attempt to surge ahead of a pack; also known as a *flyer.*

carbon fiber: A material containing special resins that allow reshaping when heated; used in molded boots.

double-push: An advanced speed skating stroke utilizing a pull with the recovering leg.

drafting: Skating in a paceline within the slipstream of another skater to reduce wind resistance and conserve energy.

fartlek: Swedish for "speed play"; a training technique that mixes up a variety of intensities or training methods in a continuous single session.

hawking the line: Thrusting the lead skate over the finish line.

lactate: A byproduct of anaerobic training that causes burning and may lead to cramping in muscle tissues.

paceline: A pack of skaters in single-file drafting cooperatively.

(continued on next page)

Few sights are as elegant as a fast-moving paceline of speed skaters, sleek legs stroking in synchronized rhythm, colorful torsos curled forward almost spoon-fashion close. Though these skaters still make up only a single-digit percentage of the total in-line family, their numbers are steadily growing and with them, speed skating opportunities and prize purses.

Below the elite level—where cash prizes support only a few full-time pros—others race for the pure joy of competition or to gain the fitness and technique benefits that come from race training. All who participate ultimately become winners, because speed skating teaches the value of teamwork while rewarding individuals who are disciplined and organized about pursuing their goals.

Dedicated fitness skaters are well qualified for outdoor in-line competitions. Anybody who has developed good stroke technique (see chapter 2) and works out with a regular skate training program (see chapter 3) is ready to consider entering a speed skating event. To encourage such folks, many races include fitness and recreation divisions and award prizes to the top finishers.

History and Organization

Americans have been racing on wheeled footwear since the first recorded speed competition in 1938. With today's superior five-wheel in-line skates, athletes all over the world continue to break speed records in a variety of race venues both indoors and out. Faced with in-line's domination over quad skates in speed events in the mid-1990s, USA Roller Skating (USA/RS), speed skating's domestic governing body, created separate divisions for roller and in-line racers to keep a fair level of competition in

DIALECT *(continued from previous page)*

race pace skating: Solo training at race pace.
tapering: A strategy for achieving maximum recovery by race day without losing peak conditioning.

sanctioned meets and at national championships. The governing organization for international events, the Federation Internationale de Roller Skating, went a step further; it sanctions races on in-line skates only.

Gear

Speed skating can be expensive. Don't let that stop you from participating but do try to find a balance between the money you have to spend and the value you place on having a competitive edge.

Speed Boots

Speed boots feature a low cuff to allow a deeper forward flex and more range of motion for the ankle. The combination of longer frames and a fifth wheel translates to more pushing traction, results in longer glides, and improves stability at high speeds. There are three approaches to getting into

Keith Sutter

Ready-made speed skates.

a pair of five-wheel skates: purchasing off-the-shelf skates, assembling prebuilt components you select individually, or ordering a totally custom boot-and-component setup.

Which method is right for you? Start with fit: A skate model with no customizable fit features is apt to be comfortable for only 20 percent of the population. The heat molding available in some fitness skates and prebuilt boots might satisfy 40 percent of the population, while full-boot heat molding capabilities increases the likelihood of a fit for up to 60 percent. The remaining folks with "special" feet must resort to the more expensive, fully customized boots.

OFF THE SHELF

The most popular skate manufacturers carry their own speed skates, sometimes equipped with a removable heel brake. Five-wheel fitness skates fall into this category, too. The most popular U.S. brands are Salomon, K2, Miller, Rollerblade, and Roces. Prices start at about $300.

Comfort is still just as important as with other types of in-line skates, but with high-end racing boots it is a bit more elusive. With less padding, there's a fine line between "snug enough for precision" and "too small." The lower (or missing) cuff provides less ankle support, which requires good balance and a combination of hip and ankle muscles to remain upright. After several hours of skating on rough surfaces, muscles around the shins and ankles can become painfully tired, and even a pair of heat-molded boots could cause bruising if not properly fitted.

ASSEMBLING COMPONENTS

Selecting prebuilt components lets you build a semicustom pair of speed skates with parts that can be upgraded or swapped at will. Expect to pay up to $1,000 for good quality parts.

When choosing a prebuilt speed boot, decide first whether you will be skating outdoors or indoors and whether you want a short-track, long-track, or hybrid boot. It's best to discuss this with a

HOME HEAT MOLDING

Never try heating boots in an oven or microwave. Perform this more gentle procedure only on leather or synthetic leather boots, and at your own risk.

1. Buy a turkey-basting bag at the grocery store and have on hand a pot large and deep enough to accommodate your boot (without frames and wheels).

2. Determine by feel where you need adjustments inside the boot.

3. Remove the frame if possible, laces, and brake (if any) from each boot.

4. Put a boot into the bag, and then push part of the bag inside the boot so hot water can be next to the inside of the boot without getting it wet. Secure the top of the bag to be sure water won't make direct contact with the boot.

5. Submerge the bagged boot in a pot of boiling water for about 4 minutes. Make sure the boot remains completely dry inside the bag.

6. Remove the boot from the pot and the bag. Pull aside the tongue and press a hammer handle hard against the inside at the point where your foot needs more space. At the same time, press a cold, wet towel on the outside of that spot and hold it in place for 2 minutes. The coldness will set the adjustment you make to the leather. You have about 30 to 60 seconds to make an adjustment before the boot cools down.

7. Put on the skate and see how it feels. If further adjustments are necessary, repeat the above bagging, heating, and pressing steps until you've corrected the fit.

---

speed coach, experienced speed skate outfitters, or knowledgeable sales reps.

- The **short-track boot** shell is made of lightweight but strong moldable material, such as Kevlar or carbon fiber, and features a rigid cuff that encases the ankles.

- **Long-track boots** are designed for marathons and come with a lower cuff for more ankle flexibility. They also feature a hard sole and moldable "counters" (internal lateral-support pieces) with a leather upper.

- **Hybrid racing boots** combine the lower cuff and sleeker design of a long-track boot with the supportive carbon fiber shell of a short-track boot. These are versatile enough to accommodate both

indoor and outdoor events as well as short- and long-track in-line and ice races.

One component of a semicustom setup.

Simmons

Custom

Many speed professionals skate on custom-molded boots and prebuilt frames mounted to their own specifications and biomechanics, using specialized wheels and bearings.

Custom boots are created from a plaster cast or outline of the skater's foot. Due to the expense, these are best left to skaters with special foot problems who can't get a proper fit otherwise. Generally, the companies that perform this service will also configure the boot with the requested ankle height, thickness, type of frame mount hardware and, of course, color.

See the sidebar on page 89 for a clever boot-fitting method used by Howard Cohen, a dedicated San Francisco skater and organizer of the SF-Skaters e-mail list, a popular communication medium for the Bay Area (sfskaters@sfskaters.org).

Tip: If you need to adjust the inside arch, do this first with a full water submersion. Then, leave the arch out of the water when you submerge other areas to be adjusted, so it doesn't spring back before you're finished fitting the boot.

When selecting prebuilt components or planning for a custom boot, get advice from an experienced speed skater or coach for help in determining what best suits your goals and capabilities.

Frames

Speed skating frames are made from aircraft-grade aluminum. Standard frame length is 12.8 inches, but taller skaters (over 6'2") may go up to 13.5 inches to compensate for the slightly slower stroke cadence of their longer legs.

Speed frames can vary in height by as much as half an inch. A lower profile is more stable and has better wheel-feel, but high profile frames are believed to furnish a longer push displacement and better boot clearance during hard turns.

Mount the frame on your boot with as much wheel extending out in front of the toe as there is behind the heel. Center it so the front wheel will be lined up between the first two toes and the back wheel is positioned very slightly toward the inside of the heel. Ideally, when you stand with your weight evenly distributed over both feet your skates will tip slightly onto the outside edges. If your ankles tip inward, shift the frame a millimeter or two toward the arch.

Frame position is a highly individual preference, and the tiniest shift at toe or heel could either vastly improve your stroke or cause pain. Before you start thinking that all of your problems stem from frame positioning, get advice from an experienced coach, speed skater, or qualified shop personnel.

Wheels

Speed wheels range from 76 mm to 82 mm in diameter. The taller the wheels, the faster you roll. A harder wheel (83–85A durometer) reduces rolling

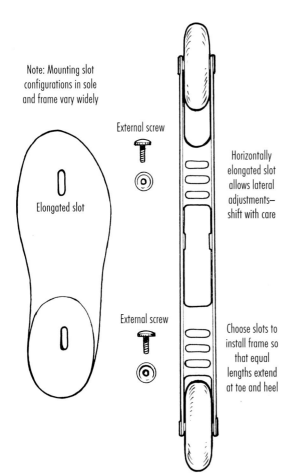

Note: Mounting slot configurations in sole and frame vary widely

External screw

Elongated slot

Horizontally elongated slot allows lateral adjustments—shift with care

External screw

Choose slots to install frame so that equal lengths extend at toe and heel

Frame placement.

resistance, and a narrow profile reduces wheel friction from contact with the pavement. Spoked hubs make the wheels lighter and faster and help keep bearings cool at high speeds. To ensure your fastest times on race day, install new wheels to eliminate the drag of wheels that have been worn to a flatter profile. (See the wheel-profiling product Wheel Hog listed in the Speed Skating Resources section at the end of this chapter.)

Bearings

Don't rely on your choice of bearings to guarantee faster times. Most skaters know that the higher the ABEC number, the more precisely a bearing is made. But because ABEC ratings were designed to dictate manufacturing tolerances for bearings used in machinery at much higher revolutions than skating (up to 2,600 rpm for skating versus 10,000 + rpm for machinery), it's debatable whether an ABEC 5 bearing spins noticeably faster than an ABEC 3, even though you might pay up to a dollar more per bearing.

To get the maximum advantage from your bearings,

- Buy good quality, high-precision bearings with removable shields to allow cleaning.

- Clean and lubricate bearings frequently to keep out the grit and extend bearing life. Prior to every race, clean them and lubricate with a light oil (see page 12).

- Improve your skating technique!

Skinsuits

In-line racers gain a competitive edge by wearing Lycra skinsuits that allow freedom of movement while eliminating wind resistance from a flapping T-shirt or baggy shorts. These usually are made of wicking fabrics to help keep the skin dry. Pro skaters' sponsors supply skinsuits covered with manufacturer logos. Individuals or club teams can order custom-made uniforms from a variety of companies that advertise in the back pages of magazines such as *Fitness and SpeedSkating Times*.

SkidSkins makes bike-style shorts and full-length stretch pants from a breathable, abrasion-resistant fabric to protect the skin in the event of a sliding fall. Boot covers made of the same material are also available. (See the Speed Skating Resources at the end of this chapter).

Protective Gear

USA/RS speed event rules require a properly fitted and safety-rated helmet with its chin strap fastened. For protection and comfort that won't slow you down, buy a lightweight, well-vented model with an aerodynamic shape. See the Helmet Primer on page 14 for details about current helmet standards and advice for getting a proper fit. Wrist guards are also required in some events.

Speed skaters tend to leave pads behind to reduce wind drag and interference with stroke technique, and most of them sport at least one battle scar as evidence. Until you have attained the quick and nimble balance that helps elite racers avoid crashes, you should continue to wear wrist guards or—at the very least—protect your palms with padded, abrasion-resistant gloves (use bike gloves or aggressive skating gloves with a wrist wrap). There is no reason for fitness and recreational skaters to race unprotected.

Race Formats

Every year, hundreds of races are held across North America, making it easy for anybody with a competitive side to find speed skating opportunities nearby.

Outdoor Racing

Most domestic races are outdoors, ranging in length from 5 to 100 kilometers but most often 10 kilometers (6.23 miles). Besides a pro/elite and advanced class, many races include divisions for fitness skaters who are allowed to compete on either four-or five-wheel skates. Marathons of 40 k (24.92 miles) or longer have become very popular, and the well-organized annual Northshore Marathon in Duluth is widely acclaimed as U.S. skaters' favorite. Outdoor race types include

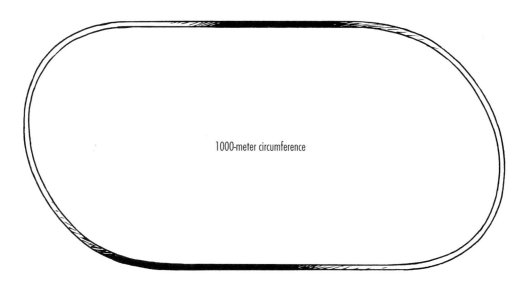

1000-meter circumference

Indoor "oval" used by USA/RS.

Circuit race: An outdoor road race run on a closed loop anywhere from 1,500 to 4,000 meters (4 km) per lap.

Criterium: An outdoor race run on a 1,000- to 2,000-meter loop road or course.

Elimination: A lap race used to weed out the slowest skaters in order to reduce the field of competitors.

Heat race: A qualifying race to narrow the field of competitors.

Out-and-back race: An outdoor road course that starts and ends at the same point.

Points race: A 10,000-meter (men's) or 5,000-meter (women's) international event where the top finishers of individual laps and the race itself earn points according to placing.

Point-to-point race: An outdoor road course that starts at one point and ends at another.

Time trial: A 300-meter solo sprint against the clock rather than other competitors.

Outdoor courses are further characterized by local street configurations, quality of asphalt, grades, and turns. USA/RS runs races that serve as qualifiers for international events, following standard rules and formats for either road or track.

In road races, point-to-point or **open courses** are most often used for marathons. **Closed-circuit courses** utilize a counterclockwise loop that can accommodate lap-based races from 300 meters to 20 kilometers in length. Outdoor track events are held on a **parabolic loop** of 150 to 300 meters with banked corners and a smooth skating surface.

Indoor Racing

USA/RS sanctions indoor races on an unbanked, asymmetrical 100-meter track. The smooth surface is either wood or concrete and is coated with a clear finish to provide good wheel grip. Racers compete in 14 age- and gender-based divisions. Boys and girls compete together through age 15 in the Primary, Juvenile, Elementary, Freshman, and Sophomore divisions. They are divided by gender in the Junior, Senior, Classic, and Masters divisions. Veteran men and women are once again combined in the 45-and-over division. Each division races three distances determined by age and gender, with the longest being 3,000 meters (senior men).

Contestants earning the highest number of points advance from local to regional contests and ultimately compete in the Indoor Speed Skating National Championships held in late July or early

ROLL MODEL

Racing on skates is empowering. When you feel strong and healthy in your body, you feel strong and healthy in your life. Racing sharpens and tunes your body, your mind, and the communication between the two.

Race training yields benefits that affect all areas of your life. Set goals you can live with—challenge yourself but don't hurt yourself. Listen to your body and make taking care of it a priority in your training. No race is worth harming yourself physically.

Speed skating is a very technical sport that involves much more than just physical conditioning. When you develop good technique, you can go faster with less work. Good race strategy can put you ahead of someone who is in better condition. A race is simply an opportunity to demonstrate what you can do at that time. Your only real competition is yourself.

Skating gives me great feelings of freedom, grace, power, and of being alive. I love the speed and the fluid sensation of gliding over pavement, the camaraderie of skating with friends, and the sense of adventure, play, and connection to nature that comes from training outdoors.

—Anna Stubbs, former ultramarathon racer and X Games competitor; winner of the 138-mile Fresno-to-Bakersfield race; cofounder of Roller Divas, a women's speed skating club; On-a-Roll SkateSchool founder and instructor

August. Two- and four-person relay teams also advance to the U.S. Championships based on local and regional placing. The top national skaters have earned highly revered titles by the time they represent the United States at the international World Championships.

Federation Internationale de Roller Skating (FIRS) governs the annual World Championships and the Pan American Games. In these competitions, solo 300-meter time trials determine heat placement for the 500- and 1,500-meter races. Elimination races and qualifying heats serve to identify the competitors who will advance to the final rounds. The 10,000-meter is a points race, the 20,000-meter uses elimination races to determine the winner, and international marathons are raced pack style.

Key Skills

If possible, join a local speed skating club to work on technique, drafting, and race strategy. In a group, you'll get a great workout while you pol-

ish your competitive attitude and learn to pace yourself for a long race. You will also gain the necessary experience to skate with confidence in a paceline. Club members will be able to refer you to a speed coach or clinics if you feel you need more one-on-one instruction, and they'll share their opinions on gear purchases.

As with most very technical kinetic movement, the more you learn about good stroke technique, the more you discover you need to learn! That dangling carrot at the end of the stick is one of the most compelling aspects of speed skating. The stroke technique pointers below are merely a summary of what is available in excellent books such as Barry Publow's *Speed on Skates* and Dianne Holum's *The Complete Handbook of Speed Skating*, favorites of speed skaters everywhere.

The popular double-push is an advanced and technically complicated stroke that is beyond the scope of this introductory chapter. However, the Speed Skating Resources section at the end of this chapter lists videos, books, and workshops for those interested in gaining this race-winning skill.

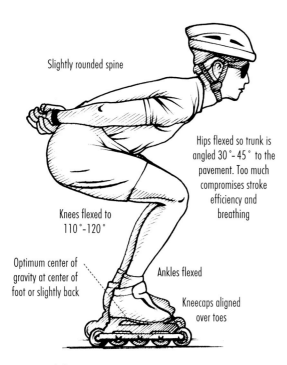

Slightly rounded spine

Hips flexed so trunk is angled 30°-45° to the pavement. Too much compromises stroke efficiency and breathing

Knees flexed to 110°-120°

Optimum center of gravity at center of foot or slightly back

Ankles flexed

Kneecaps aligned over toes

Basic speed skating position.

Stroke Technique

If you're serious about entering the world of racing, your form should already incorporate the following.

- **Body position:** A deep tuck reduces wind resistance and enables you to exert greater force when extending the leg to stroke. Strive for a 110-degree bend at the knee with your torso angled at 30 to 45 degrees to the ground. Round your shoulders and upper spine slightly forward to reduce lower back aching.

- **Arms:** Reduce wind resistance and conserve energy by learning to skate with both hands behind your back. For a one-arm swing on a straightaway, swing from front to back with the palm facing toward your body. A two-arm swing, used primarily for short bursts of hard effort, requires a slightly more side-to-side movement.

- **Stroke:** Speed skating technique starts with solid mastery of the power stride described in chapter 2: a full-length push that is perpendicular to the direction of travel with all of the wheels generating force against the pavement for as long a stroke as possible.

Your speed technique training should focus on each of the four stroke phases: push-off, glide, recovery, and set-down. Weight transfer awareness is just as important.

Push-off is the long, accelerating stroke that is the source of forward propulsion in the classic speed skating stroke.

- Start pushing from a 110-degree knee bend and end at full leg extension with a pronounced heel kick.

- Initiating the push from a tuck with well-flexed hips, knees, and ankles contributes to a powerful extension.

- The push starts on the support leg's outside wheel edges and ends on the inside edges.

- Power comes from the first one-third of the push as the stroking skate rolls from its outside edges over the wheel apex and onto the inside edges.

PRACTICE TIP

If you tend to flick with the toe at the end of each stroke, concentrate on pushing the right heel wheel toward a two o'clock position and the left toward ten o'clock. This overcompensation will result in more success at pushing at 90 degrees from the direction of travel.

Glide is the time spent rolling on just one skate. Road friction and bearing limitations reduce speed during the glide—that's why in-line stroke tempo is slightly higher than the tempo for ice skating.

- Glide on the outside wheel edges of the support skate.

- During the glide, you are regrouping the other skate for a new push.

- The glide becomes a push at the moment the regrouped skate is set down and weight transfer to that skate is completed.

PRACTICE TIP

Try gliding on one skate's center edge as far as possible to improve balance and hip strength. To regain momentum, use scooters to push with the other skate (see page 42). Gradually work toward gliding for long distances on the outside edge, with and without scooters.

Recovery is the act of drawing the leg that just stroked back under the body to prepare for set-down.

- Keep the recovering skate close to the pavement to avoid wasting energy.

- To avoid pushing off the toe wheel, keep all wheels parallel to the pavement as well as to the direction of travel.

- The toe wheel traces a semicircle behind you to return slightly toe-in and close to the support skate. (See the diagram on page 25.)

- Literally recover by relaxing your leg muscles so blood can flow to flush away lactate buildup.

PRACTICE TIP

At lift-off, consciously keep the ankle flexed forward (or lift your toes inside the boot) to better steer the toe of your skate through its proper semicircular route.

Set-down is the most dynamic moment of the stroke because it initiates weight transfer and the beginning of a new push.

- Drive the recovering knee forward so you can set down slightly ahead of the support leg.

- Land on the outside edges of your wheels.

- After a forceful side-directed push with the opposite skate, the moment of set-down is similar to the feeling of catching yourself after tipping to the side.

PRACTICE TIP

To improve your outside edge set-down, work on a more powerful, side-directed push that can shove the hips laterally toward and beyond the recovering skate.

Weight transfer begins at the moment of set-down.

- Your weight moves from the support skate's outside edges (set-down and glide), briefly across the center edges (push), and onto the inside edges (extension).

- Shifting your center of gravity laterally compounds the pressure on your pushing edges and saves precious energy.

- Strong hip muscles produce the stability that maximizes push effectiveness.

PRACTICE TIP

After a forceful push that shifts your weight toward the recovery skate, delay set-down until you feel you are about to fall to the side.

Cornering

Crossovers are important for all types of racing, because they are used to maintain or even gain speed through a corner. Track skaters become experts at counterclockwise turns but lack versatility without the ability to turn clockwise. Right-handed people prefer to turn left and usually find that clockwise crossovers require more practice.

The crossover presents a significant challenge to inexperienced racers, because it requires the skater to lean the upper body and center of gravity momentarily outside the stable space between both feet. Early crossover practice is best done on a marked circle such as those found on school playgrounds. Alternatively, place an object on the pavement that can serve as a center marker for spotting.

The following is a progression of skills performed while skating in a circle, culminating in successful crossover turns. Because more speed skaters need help cornering to the right than to the left, the following instructional sequence teaches crossovers in the clockwise direction. If you fail at any point, return to your last successful step and drill longer on the subsequent moves until you can achieve at least a couple laps of crossovers.

1. Begin swizzling around the circle at a moderate speed, traveling in a clockwise direction. (See Forward Swizzles on page 42.)

2. Transition to scooters: Push with your left skate's inside wheel edges while gliding on the right support leg. (See Scooters on pages 42–43.) Rotate the shoulders, hips, and torso toward the center of the circle.

3. Modify the scooters so you are returning the left skate to the pavement directly in front of the right along the circle's perimeter line. Continue for a lap or two, but be sure to retain that inward upper body rotation.

4. Still doing scooters with the left skate, relax your right ankle so the right skate can tip onto its outside edge. Combined with the upper body rotation, this forces your upper body to tilt slightly into the circle.

5. Coinciding with a left skate lift-off, the weight transfer changes the right skate's glide into a push on the outside edges that passes under your body and away from the center of the circle. Your thighs are crossed because the outside (left) skate is in place for set-down.

6. Immediately after the left skate set-down, recover the right skate, move your knee forward, and set the wheels down on their outside edges.

7. Continue circling, now concentrating on equal force and rhythm as you push with both skates, keeping your wheels close to the pavement. The more successful your crossovers, the faster you'll go.

Cornering with crossovers.

 PRACTICE TIP

To correct twisting the shoulders away from turn direction, keep your eyes fixed on the center of the circle or imagine hugging it with your left hand ahead and your right hand behind.

8. Gradually assume an aerodynamic tuck by folding the inside (right) arm behind while swinging the outside (left) arm back during the crossunder push.

PRACTICE TIP

Stop stroking and coast out of the circle if you find yourself moving too fast for comfort or beginning to feel dizzy.

FIGURE EIGHTS

You can strengthen both directions of your forward crossover turns and improve your outside edge skills by tracing figure eights around a pair of real or imaginary 30-foot-diameter adjacent circles. Skating in a counterclockwise direction around the first circle, begin making crossovers. Focus your eyes left toward the direction of the turn. Do not rotate your hips away from the perimeter of the circle. As you complete a lap around the first circle, change direction with one or two straight forward glides to start skating clockwise around the second circle. Turn your head to the right when making clockwise turns. Tilt your upper body into the circles for easier crossovers.

Skating without a Brake

Whatever you do, if you have developed that all-important instinctive dependence on the heel brake so strongly encouraged in the first half of this book, don't wear your new five-wheel skates outside a protected environment until you have a full arsenal of secondary stopping abilities. In my experience, it was humbling to feel that old creeping fear as I accelerated unwillingly to a speed that would have felt quite safe if only I was wearing a heel brake. Appreciate this very appropriate fear and then learn all the techniques you can to skate safely without a brake. Several methods for surviving brakeless are covered in

- Hill Skills, page 28
- Slowing Down and Stopping, page 129

Starting Line Survival

Except for the 300-meter sprint, most races begin with a mass start. While the world-class competitors avoid the worst of the crush because they're at the front, the rest of the pack can end up scrambling in a sea of flashing frames for a good position. The chances are high for tripping over the skate of somebody pushing with the opposite foot.

Do your best to surround yourself with others of similar ability at the starting line. That way, once the starting signal sounds, you won't be immediately presented with the need to pass or be passed. A wide arm swing can clear more space around you. Stay low to improve your balance and center of gravity, but start the race with short, quick strokes to keep your skates under your body until there's enough room for your normal stride.

Drafting

Drafting other skaters within a paceline not only helps you conserve energy, it also helps everybody in the group skate 20 to 30 percent faster than if they were skating alone. A successful paceline is the result of maintaining a consistent speed and frequently rotating a fresh lead skater to the front to break the wind and pull the rest of the group. Key points to good drafting are

- **Effective distance**: To skate within the "wind tunnel" of the skater ahead, stay as close as possible without risking contact. Your chin should be over his or her hips.

- **Synchronized strokes**: Mimic the stroke length and cadence of the lead skater exactly to ensure that your body and limbs remain within that skater's wind shadow. If you fall out of synch, extend one glide a few seconds, take several short, quick strides, or push twice with the same leg.

- **Sharing the workload**: The more skaters in the group, the more frequently you should rotate the leader out of pulling

Jeff Dowling, courtesy of *Fitness and SpeedSkating Times*

Drafting in a paceline.

position. With more than five people, leaders should rotate back after about 30 strokes. Without changing tempo, step abruptly to the side of the paceline so the next skater can take over, then stroke slightly less forcefully to drop back, sticking close to the line. You won't click skates as long as your strokes remain in synch. The new leader resists the urge to surge and instead concentrates on maintaining the original tempo and speed.

○ **Handling speed variations:** Constantly monitor the pack ahead to conserve energy that might be wasted playing catch-up. To deal with a slow-down, stop stroking and place the back of your hand lightly against the next skater's back (to prevent grabbing his or her clothes). As the pack compresses, minimize the impact by allowing your elbow to bend so it can absorb the momentum. Try not to push the skater ahead and, if that can't be helped, direct the pressure so you push only gently forward. Once the paceline resumes accelera-

tion, allow a bit of extra space to open up briefly so you have enough room to accelerate back into the draft.

○ **Pack strategy:** Besides monitoring your own pack, in a race situation you must also position yourself strategically in the middle of the field or toward the front so you can respond instantly to a breakaway. Glance over your shoulder frequently and keep tabs on your competitors by learning to read their body language.

If you harbor fears about skating in a tight pack,

○ Get used to drafting by skating behind an understanding friend; grip the fingers of your friend's hand nestled palm-up on his or her lower back.

○ Find a few like-minded friends and build your confidence and trust by skating in a paceline as often as possible.

○ Learn to mimic a variety of skating styles.

- Be very predictable, to make drafting easier on those behind you.

- Skate solo and choose shorter events to make up for the extra energy demands.

Breakaway

A breakaway, also known as a *flyer*, is the act of sprinting to break out of a wind-protected draft and put distance between yourself and other competitors. The purpose of a midrace breakaway is either to advance solo ahead of the pack or to tire them by forcing a chase. Near the end of a race, a terminal breakaway is an all-out attempt to leave everybody else in your dust as you cross the finish line alone.

As a strategic move for the solo skater, timing a breakaway is everything. A well-planned attack takes into consideration current course topography (avoid downhill breakaways where pack speed is faster), pack attention span (are they tired? distracted by rough pavement?), and the positions and status of nearby competitors. Start sprinting quietly from a point well back of those you need to pass to gain the element of surprise and precious acceleration time. Skate a diagonal path away from the paceline to make it harder for them to slip into your draft and delay notice from those up front.

Utilize a high-tempo stroke and swing both arms for added speed. Remember this, though: Because a sprint is an anaerobic activity, you can endure less than a minute of this type of energy before lactic acid buildup begins its muscular burn.

Race Training

Choosing the First Race

We've all got to start somewhere, right? To make your debut in speed skating as painless as possible, start with a realistic goal when choosing that first race, preferably an event that is compatible with your areas of strength. If you're great at sprinting, set your sights on training for a track competition where you can race in a 500 meter. A 10-kilometer road race (6.23 miles) is a good first race and the most frequently offered event. The promoter's registration forms cover location and time, prizes, class divisions, other race day activities, entrance fees, and participation requirements.

Designing Your Program

Pro speed skaters reach top ranks because they are organized, focused, and disciplined. An entry-level racer can take advantage of those attributes, too, by setting specific goals and then following a schedule for reaching them. When planning for a race season, an electronic calendar or spreadsheet program is a great tool to keep you on track.

Map out a month-by-month, phased program that builds the following in the sequence listed.

1. aerobic fitness (cardio training)

2. muscular strength and endurance (aerobics and resistance training)

3. anaerobic recovery (interval training)

4. explosive power (plyometric exercises)

You should already be following a regular conditioning program to improve your aerobic fitness, muscular strength and endurance, and anaerobic capacity. These training methods, along with plyometrics, are described in chapter 3. But if you actually want to *win* a race, you need to create a phased seasonal training plan that results in planned incremental adaptations in these areas and includes the exercises that build explosive sport-specific power.

Block out a training plan by working backward from your selected race date. If you're planning to enter multiple races, or if the chosen event is near the end of the season, break down the months into three phases: early season (build up a base), mid- to late season (work on endurance and strength conditioning), and the final six weeks (build speed and power). Next, block out the first two weeks of the first phase's training plan. About 14 days later, start working on the new two-week plan based on your progress. Continue to chart your training plans in two-week increments through all phases. And to keep your chances for injury low, don't slack off on those warm-ups, stretches, and cool-downs.

- Early-season workouts should build aerobic and muscular endurance so you can skate longer and faster without tiring and build resilience for the demands of harder training later on. At this time it is appropriate to use cross training to diversify your cardio workouts. Begin an easy resistance training program with loads you can lift 15 to 20 times using the largest muscles in your legs, back, and chest. Advance over the weeks from one set each for these three areas to three sets of two or three different exercises for each muscle group.

- At midseason, or when your race is still two months away, begin gradually increasing the volume and intensity of your cardio and weight training work. Add a weekly hard-skating interval session. Also schedule in two or three medium cardio days (either work on stroke technique or skate long, slow distances) and one hard day (sprint and hill work; intervals). After three to four weeks, increase your intervals to two days per week and make the medium and hard days harder by skating longer and working at higher training heart rates. Be sure to do all your interval training on skates; this actually develops new capillaries in your legs that can remove lactate buildup more quickly and help you successfully endure a long breakaway effort. To keep from overtraining, include one easy day per week (complete rest or very light cross training). Always follow hard days with an easy one and never do two hard days in a row.

- Six weeks before race day, advanced athletes can safely begin to add plyometric exercises and after a month can do them at the end of weight training workouts. Drop any nonskate training to no more than 20 percent of workout time. Start training at a race pace, one you can sustain nonstop over a distance that is at least half the length of your chosen event. It's a great workout and gives you the confidence that you can complete at least half your intended race at your best speed.

- A week before race day, begin to back off on training intensity to make sure you will be fully primed for peak performance. For example, take a rest day on Sunday; then over the next four days skate in sessions no more than half an hour long in which you skate hard 1-minute intervals followed by 5 minutes of rest. Do five interval/rest cycles the first day, four the second, and so on, decreasing to two sets on the last day. Then do absolutely nothing for one or two days before the race.

The Big Day

On race day, don't make the common novice mistake of burning out early from putting your heart and soul into the first half of the race. Pace yourself and have confidence in your preparation. Your determination and focus will pay off no matter how you place in the race. By putting yourself through a speed skater's training regimen, you have blossomed into an elite athlete.

Dan Kibler

Fitness skater completing a marathon.

SPEED SKATING RESOURCES

ORGANIZATIONS

Federation Internationale
de Roller Skating (FIRS)
Rambla Catalunya 121
Piso 6, Puerta 7
08008 Barcelona, Spain
Isidro Oliveras, President
34-93-2377055
fax 34-93-2372733
www.firs.org
International governing body for
speed skating.

USA Roller Skating
(USA/RS)
P.O. Box 6579
4730 South St.
Lincoln NE 68506
402-483-7551
fax 402-483-1465
E-mail: usacrs@usacrs.com
www.usacrs.com
Domestic governing body promoting roller sports via training,
team support, and sanctioned
hockey, artistic, and speed
skating competitions.

USA Inline Racing (USA/IR)
1271 Boynton #15
Glendale CA 91205
Phone and fax 818-548-8559
Rick Babington, Vice President
of Operations
E-mail: usairvpops@aol.com
www.usainline.org
Membership association to
promote outdoor in-line racing
at all levels and organizers of
the National Points Circuit
(NPC).

National In-Line Racing
Association (NIRA)
4708 E. 4th Place
Tulsa OK 74112
Joe Cotter, Executive Director
800-SK8 NIRA/800-758-6472
fax 918-627-3504
E-mail: NIRA@aol.com
www.sk8nira.com
Indoor league and organizer of
the Annual Racing Series, producing competitions following the format of international short-track
speed races.

PUBLICATIONS

*The Complete Handbook of Speed
Skating.* Dianne Holum. Hillside
NJ: Enslow, 1984.
*Fitness and SpeedSkating Times
Magazine*
2910 N.E. 11th Ave.
Pompano Beach FL 33064
305-782-5928
E-mail: speedsk8in@aol.com
www.speedsk8in.com
Jumping into Plyometrics. Donald
Chu. Champaign IL: Human
Kinetics, 1998.
*Speed on Skates: A Complete Tech-
nique, Training, and Racing
Guide for In-Line and Ice
Skaters.* Barry Publow. Cham-
paign IL: Human Kinetics, 1999.
*Strength and Power Training for
Speed Skaters.* Barry Publow.
Ottawa: Breakaway Speed
Specialists, 1998.

VIDEOS

*Secrets of the Double-Push Tech-
nique.* Barry Publow. Ottawa:

Breakaway Speed Specialists,
1998.

WORKSHOPS

Take a weekend to learn the double-push with author, coach, and
former Canadian World Team
member **Barry Publow**. Besides
intensive double-push instruction,
the two-day clinics address dry-
land training methods, hills and
cornering, and pack and breakaway strategies. Each participant
receives a video analysis of his or
her technique, a T-shirt, and a
copy of Publow's video, *Secrets of
the Double-Push Technique* (613-
725-1290, e-mail: breakaway@
igs.net, <www.igs.net/
~breakaway/clinics.htm>).

The **Eddy Matzger Workshop** is
a weekend clinic for all abilities,
teaching skating and racing techniques including the double-push,
through group skates, games and
drills, off-skate exercises, mock
stage races, and video analysis.
Workshops are scheduled across
the United States every year and
are listed on the website (888-
WRK-SHOP/888-975-7467,
e-mail: workshop@gte.net,
<www.snapsite.com/guests/
sk8ctrl/public/html/page29.html>).

WEBSITES

<www.home.att.net/~bsracing/
nims1.htm> National In-line
Masters Series (NIMS);
promoters of a race series
(continued on next page)

SPEED SKATING RESOURCES *(continued from previous page)*

designed for Masters skaters (35 years or older) competing on a national level. <*www.wheelhog.com*> Home site of the Wheel Hog, a reshaping tool that can restore the wheel profile for speed, hockey, and aggressive skate wheels. <*www.roadskating.com*> Road-skating International is a membership organization devoted to providing information, event opportunities, and links to help popularize the sport through a community of racers, event promoters, and sponsors.

CHAPTER EIGHT

ROLLER HOCKEY

DIALECT

blade: The curved portion at the bottom of the hockey stick that is used to pass, stick handle, or shoot the puck; usually plastic for roller hockey.

blocker: The square pad attached to the glove the goalie uses to hold his or her stick.

boards: The markers (barriers, line, and so on) that define the perimeter of the rink.

box strategy (diamond): Defensive tactic where skaters defend the goal in a box or diamond formation to keep the attacking team and the puck outside and thwart scoring attempts.

breakout strategy: A coordinated plan to rapidly move the puck to the opposition's end of the court and beat them to their goal.

C-cutting: Backward propulsion achieved by sculling the skates in a backward arc; independent-foot backward swizzles.

continued on next page

Hockey gave birth to in-line skating as we know it today, and roller hockey has played a big part in fueling a steady worldwide growth in the number of folks on wheels. Millions of passionate participants see themselves first as hockey players and second as skaters. The game, the teamwork, the puck, the score—this is what's important! When you first start playing, your abilities to pass, shoot, and drive the puck down the court will seem to emerge without conscious effort because of the game's intrinsic fast-paced excitement.

But of course your skills will grow faster and better if you do pay conscious attention to learning all you can to become an excellent player. This chapter will help you bone up on the specifics of the game, court, equipment, and positions. And almost more importantly, it lists suggestions for the best videos and books to learn the skills you need to become a respectable hockey player. Whether or not you have mastered all the moves described in chapter 2, these resources will give you an excellent start in the game of roller hockey.

As in any sport, safety comes first. Enlist the expert advice of a qualified professional to outfit yourself with the necessary gear and use qualified instructional videos, books, and clinics to improve your skills. Remember that the better you become, the more you will appreciate and learn to love the game of roller hockey. Have fun!

History and Organization

Roller hockey was a popular sport as long ago as 1936, when the first men's World Championship was played on quads (traditional roller skates). But it was a pair of ice hockey players who brought the game to its new level of popularity. In the mid 1980s, Scott

DIALECT *continued from previous page*

center court: The exact center of the playing area.

checking: Using the body to block; not allowed in amateur roller hockey.

closed blade: When the surface of the stick's blade is cupped over (tipped toward) the puck; helps keep the puck on the playing surface.

cutting the angle: Goalie position used to block the shooter's view of the net.

defensemen: Team position whose main job is to defend opposition players from encroaching to the goal.

dribble: To move the puck forward and laterally across the body using alternating light taps from both sides of the stick blade.

face-off: Initiation of play in which the referee drops the puck between two opposing forwards.

forward: Team position whose main job is to receive passes and attempt to score.

goal crease: The area within the semi-circular crease lines, including the distance from the floor to the bottom of the goal frame's cross-bar (4 vertical feet).

goal posts, net, and cross-bar: One of two framed nets into which the puck must pass to score.

goaltender: Team position whose main job is to prevent pucks from entering the goal net; also known as *goalie*.

hockey stop: A technique in which both skates are turned sharply onto their corresponding edges so that friction results in a stop. Also known as *parallel stop*.

open blade: When the surface of the stick's blade is angled away from the puck; allows the puck to be swept above the playing surface.

pass: A transfer of the puck from one player to another using the hockey stick.

penalty: A personal or technical violation of a rule, called by a referee.

poke check: Extending the hockey blade into an oncoming opponent's dribble to poke the puck away; usually performed by a backward-skating defense player.

power slide: A technique in which the skater extends one skate at an extreme angle in the direction of travel so that friction on the inside wheel edges or the skate itself results in a stop.

power stride: Forward propulsion through increased edge pressure and full leg extension starting from well-flexed knees.

power turn: A tight, swerving lunge turn made on corresponding edges in a wide scissors stance.

puck: The object used for scoring in roller hockey; this can be a disk or a ball, depending on the playing surface. A ball is better for street hockey; pucks are better for smoother surfaces.

rockering: Positioning the two center wheels slightly lower than the toe and heel wheels. The resulting arc improves quick turning ability.

save: A goalie maneuver in which different parts of the body and gear are used to stop the puck from entering the goal; variations include *body, blocker, glove, leg pad, stick, toe,* and *kick* saves.

shot: An attempt to get the puck into the opposing team's goal net.

stick: The hockey stick.

stick lift: Using the hockey stick to lift the stick of another player in order to take possession of the puck.

sweep check: Laying the shaft of the hockey stick on the surface to sweep the puck away from the oncoming player's dribble; usually done by a backward-skating defense player.

and Brennan Olson, a pair of enterprising Minnesotan ice hockey players jury-rigged the first modern version of in-line skates so they could play on pavement in the off-season. The configuration of four wheels in a straight line also gave players more speed and maneuverability than they had on quads. The invention launched not only a dynamic new team sport but a fantastic form of outdoor fun and exercise, as well.

Because roller hockey evolved from the already mature sport of ice hockey, there is no shortage of organizations supporting it at both the amateur and pro levels. Amateur organizations are listed in Roller Hockey Resources at the end of this chapter.

About the Game

The game of roller hockey is very similar to its ice-based ancestor, with the most glaring difference being that in-line hockey teams consist of four rather than five players plus a goalie. It's generally a fast-paced game with a higher goal frequency than ice hockey. Some leagues forbid checking (slamming into an opposing team member), which encourages good teamwork, technical skill, and strategy to get the puck or ball into the net and score. (For simplicity's sake, the term *puck* will be used hereafter to refer to either.)

How to Play

Depending on the league, hockey games are played in four 12-minute quarters or in two halves no longer than 15 minutes each (only actual playing time is counted). The game starts with a face-off at the center of the rink when the referee drops the puck between the sticks of two players. Members of both teams scramble to gain possession and maneuver or pass the puck down the rink close enough to their goal to attempt shooting it into the net. Each goal counts as one point, and the team with the most points after the final bell sounds is the winner.

Teams act as a four-person unit when performing defensive or offensive strategies no matter where the players are on the court. When a team loses possession of the puck, all four team members take up a defensive role. When a team gains possession of the puck, all players assume offensive play. The terms *defenseman* and *forward* denote a player's specific responsibilities during the normal course of a game.

Penalties are called when a player commits an illegal act on a member of the other team. Examples of such fouls are slashing, tripping, excessive body contact, interference, verbal abuse, rough play or fighting, and engaging in any misconduct prohibited by league rules. Penalties range from 2 minutes in the penalty box to banishment from the game, depending on the foul's seriousness. This leaves the offending player's team one person short, giving the opponents a brief advantage. The

Dan Kibler

Hockey is a fast and exciting team sport.

USA Hockey rules specify six classes of penalties: minor penalties, bench minor penalties, major penalties, misconduct penalties, match penalties, and penalty shots.

The Rink

Participants can play roller hockey on just about any smoothly paved surface. A neighborhood cul de sac, an empty parking lot, an abandoned tennis court—all are good places to play or work on stick handling and shooting skills. If space is limited, teams can play on a "half court" as is done in basketball, where a team must clear the puck across a centerline before turning to attack the goal shared by both teams. With enough interested players, the group can chip in for a pair of goal cages or assemble makeshift baseboards to keep the puck in the rink.

The regulation rink size is 200 feet long and 85 feet wide. (If necessary, a smaller court of 165

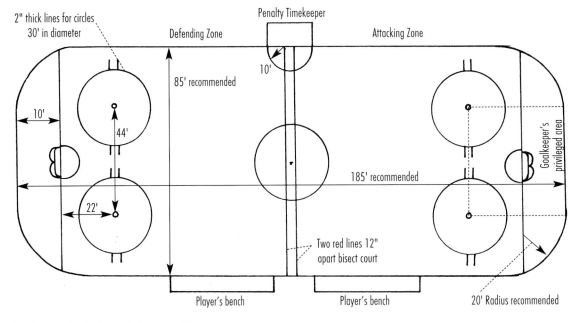

Regulation roller hockey rink (not to scale).

feet long and 65 feet wide is acceptable.) Concrete, asphalt, wood, or synthetics such as the popular Sport Court are all good playing surfaces. Each of the rink's four corners are rounded (to a 20-foot radius), and a 2-inch-thick red line bisects the rink's width into equal halves. The goal posts are centered 6 feet apart on the goal line (which divides the rink about 10 feet in from the back), and the cross-bar supports the top of the net 4 feet off the ground. The goal crease is a 6-foot-radius semicircle on the goal line marked with a 2-inch-thick red line. There is one face-off circle at the exact center of the rink and two more in each half of the rink, close to the goal, making a total of five.

A regulation rink has benches for players and officials on the sidelines, close to the centerline. A separate bench is provided for penalized players, the timekeeper, and the official scorer. Timing, scoreboard, and signal devices allow these officials to track playing time and communicate game status and scores. If boards surround the rink, they shouldn't be more than 48 inches high and should be painted white or yellow for good visibility.

Team Building

Your best resource to find out about roller hockey leagues, pickup games, or other avid players is to visit a skate shop or other sporting goods retailer that sells roller hockey equipment. (Look up "skating" in your local telephone book's yellow pages—advertisements are a big hint on who sells hockey gear.) If your town doesn't yet have such a shop, get a few friends together and organize your own team. Make it grow by posting flyers at a local skate shop; convince the manager to carry hockey equipment and support—if not sponsor—your efforts. After all, it's a win-win situation.

Contact USA Roller Skating to find the closest USA/RS-affiliated rink (see Roller Hockey Resources at the end of this chapter). The organization has been developing new hockey players and organizing league events for years. A local membership includes access to coaching education and certification. It also provides teams with banners, a quarterly newsletter, scheduling software, and technical support from both the national office and a local distributor.

To participate in regional or national roller hockey competitions, you need to hook up with a USA/RS Senior or Junior Olympic roller hockey club by contacting the regional coordinator. Senior membership includes three versions of roller hockey: Puck; North American Ball (helmets are optional and the puck is replaced by a Mylec ball); and Hardball, the original roller game utilizing canes and a hard cork or rubber ball. USA/RS organizes regional, national, and international competitions every year in which the top teams in each division play.

In the Junior Olympic program, male and female players of all ages are in development mode for the first three years so they can acquire the skills necessary at higher levels. Participants play against others of similar ability.

Positions

As the primary offensive players, the **forwards** must be fit enough to repeatedly race up and down the full length of the rink and still manage the constant sprinting required to accept passes, outmaneuver the defense, and score goals. Forwards require excellent puck handling skills to ensure successful passing, faking, and shooting. Two forwards per team are on the rink at a time: a right wing and a left wing position (unless one is in the penalty box).

Doing their best to thwart the scoring efforts of the attacking forwards, the **defensemen** try to stop incoming plays by blocking shots, stealing the puck, and passing it to their own forwards. Defensemen are experts at anticipating a forward's moves and blocking shots and passes while skating backward. A good defenseman also needs exemplary passing and shooting skills in order to move the puck to a team member at the opposite end of the rink or to shoot the puck accurately to the opposition's net. Each team has a left and a right defender on the rink at one time.

The heavily padded **goaltender** uses lightning reflexes to stop the opposing team's puck from hitting the net. Within the confines of the crease, the goaltender moves quickly from side to

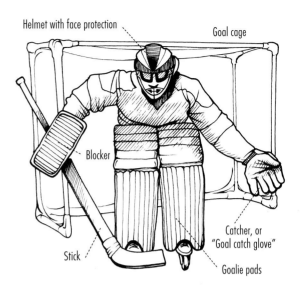

Goalie gear.

side and forward and backward to remain optimally positioned for maximum puck blocking and quick responses to the game's action. Goaltenders can also pass the puck into play.

Teams are allowed up to 10 players in uniform for a given game, including at least one substitute goalie.

Gear

Consult your local hockey shop professional to make sure you purchase the proper gear for the level of hockey you plan to play. You might need any of the following items:

- HECC-approved helmet that doesn't shift on your head. Consider getting one with a full-face shield, which some leagues require. These are lightweight even though they offer better head coverage than other types of helmets.

- Snug-fitting, hockey-specific in-lines reinforced in the toes and around the ankles to withstand constant abuse from sticks and collisions. Lace-ups make for a more custom fit and better precision in footwork.

Rick Dubrowski

Hockey skates.

- Knee and elbow pads and a pair of snug-fitting hockey gloves or other type of wrist protectors. Between the elbow pads and gloves, the forearm should be completely protected. You should be able to pick up your stick while wearing your gloves.

- A protective pelvic cup (recommended for both boys and girls).

- A mouth guard (required for all USA/RS games).

- Shin and ankle guards to protect the entire lower leg (optionally, you can integrate these into hockey-style knee pads).

- Hockey shell pants. Optional, since checking is not allowed: pants with built in hip pads or a hockey girdle with close-fitting hip, cup, kidney, and thigh pads to wear underneath.

- Lightweight shoulder pads (optional for kids).

- Goaltenders require special equipment.

Consult your local pro shop to get all the gear necessary to avoid injury.

- For indoors or games on smooth surfaces, a league-approved puck sized 1 inch thick by 3 inches across. The puck can weigh from 3.5 to 6.5 ounces.

- For street hockey, a no-bounce ball, 2.5 to 2.75 inches in diameter, weighing anywhere from 1.75 to 3 ounces.

- A hockey stick sized so that when standing in skates, you can rest the end of the stick somewhere between chin and mid-chest when the stick is balanced on the tip of the blade.. (Forwards sometimes prefer a slightly shorter measurement for easier handling; defensemen like longer sticks because they have added reach for stealing the puck.) You might need to cut a new stick to the proper length and tape the end. Beginners can buy a more forgiving stick (less curve to the blade, softer-flexing) to make learning stick handling skills a bit easier.

- The cross-bar of a standard goal cage rises 4 feet above the playing surface and is supported by a pair of goal posts 6 feet apart to which a net is attached.

Key Skills

Hockey players use the following beginner and intermediate skating skills taught by IISA-certified instructors and described in chapter 2.

- basic and power strides (Strides 2 and 3)
- backward skating
- crossovers
- lunge stop
- lunge turn
- parallel turn
- T-stop
- directional transitions

ROLL MODEL

Hockey is the greatest sport you will every play. It is fast and exciting, and it takes skill to play. I have been playing hockey since I was 6 years old, and 32 years later I still can't think of anything I would rather do than play hockey. Besides being fun to watch, hockey is a gas to participate in, whether it's on ice or an in-line court. Unlike other sports that have participants directly involved in the game for only brief moments, hockey allows all the players to be involved in the play whenever they are on the playing surface.

Aside from the sheer fun of the game, hockey is an excellent way to keep aerobically fit and to meet new friends—some who will last a lifetime. Hockey teaches you to work together with others in the pursuit of a common goal. Hockey instills "intestinal fortitude" as my dad called it—most of us call it "guts." The game will make you mentally sharper and mentally tougher, too. It will teach you how to win and lose with grace. Once you start to play hockey, I know you'll never want to stop: The better you get, the more you'll want to play.

—Bobby Hull Jr., Roller Hockey International Coach of the Year (1994), professional hockey instructor (20 years), instructional video writer, and producer and director (five videos to date)

Bobby Hull Jr., the instructional editor for *Roller Hockey* Magazine, recommends the following training videos to help you learn the techniques used by great players.

- *Roller Hockey: Skating*, produced by Robert Dean Productions, teaches basic skating and helps you improve your skills. This video is one of a series of hockey videos known for clear presentation, attention to detail, simplicity, and good quality.

- *Power Roller Hockey—Program 1: Power Skating*, also produced by Robert Dean Productions, features instructor Joe Cook, USA 2000 Olympics roller hockey team coach. This video offers great information on stick handling and passing, along with sound skating fundamentals, useful tips, and practical drills. Beginners and advanced players alike can learn the proper techniques for a hockey stop, backward skating, and crossovers.

- Bobby recommends his and Brett Hull's instructional video *Shooting and Scoring* for the best tips, demonstrations, and drills for proper shooting and scoring techniques. Covering every shot in the game, the Hulls also teach proper body position and puck position in relation to your body and the blade.

- Wayne Gretzky's and Howie Wenger's video *Train to Win: Off-Ice Fitness For High Performance Hockey* is an excellent training tool that focuses on training for power, strength, speed, agility, flexibility, recovery time, and overall performance.

Sticks in action.

Rick Dubrowski

[aq]change ref. to Hull at *RH Mag.* to current affiliation

ROLLER HOCKEY RESOURCES

ORGANIZATIONS

Roller Hockey International~
  Amateur (RHI~A)
249 E. Ocean Blvd., Suite 800
Long Beach CA 90802
310-628-0524
fax 800-884-7442
E-mail: rhi@rollerhockey.com
www.rollerhockey.com
An amateur roller hockey program
endorsed by the RHI professional
organization to develop future professionals.

USA Hockey InLine
1775 Bob Johnson Dr.
Colorado Springs CO 80906-
  4090
800-888-4656
fax 719-538-7838
E-mail: usahockeyinline@
  usahockey.org
www.usahockey.com/inline
Membership organization that
hosts regional and national championships.

USA Roller Skating (USA/RS)
P.O. Box 6579
4730 South St.
Lincoln NE 68506
George Pickard,
  Executive Director
402-483-7551
fax 402-483-1465
E-mail: usacrs@usacrs.com

www.usacrs.com
Domestic governing body promoting roller sports via training, team
support, and sanctioned hockey,
artistic, and speed skating competitions.

PUBLICATIONS

American Hockey Magazine
USA Hockey Inline
1775 Bob Johnson Dr.
Colorado Springs CO 80906-
  4090
800-888-4656
fax 719-538-7838
www.usahockey.com/news/
  subscription.htm

*California Hockey & Skating
  Magazine*
Starlight Publishing, Inc.
701J DeLong Ave.
Novato CA 94946
415-898-5414
fax 415-892-6484
E-mail: hockeyskate@aol.com

The Sports Asylum, Inc.
9018 Balboa Blvd., PMB
  Suite 575
Northridge CA 91325
800-929-2159
fax 818-895-4763
www.hockeybooks.com
40-page catalog of hockey books
and videos; reproduced online.

VIDEOS

Roller Hockey: Skating. PUBPLACE
  US: Robert Dean Productions,
  19xx (800-929-2159,
  <www.hockeybooks.com>, catalog no. R136 from Sports Asylum, Inc.).
*Power Roller Hockey—Program 1:
  Power Skating.* PUBPLACE US:
  Robert Dean Productions,
  1997 (800-929-2159,
  <www.hockeybooks.com>,
  catalog no. R160 from Sports
  Asylum, Inc.).
Shooting and Scoring. Bobby Hull
  and Brett Hull, 1999. Simi Val-
  ley CA: Albatross One, Inc.
  (800-788-1609,
  <www.shotandagoal.com>).
*Train to Win: Off-Ice Fitness For
  High Performance Hockey.*
  Wayne Gretzky and Howie
  Wenger. Westlake Village CA:
  Madacy Entertainment Group,
  1999 (800-929-2159,
  <www.hockeybooks.com>,
  catalog no. V399 from The
  Sports Asylum, Inc.).

WEBSITES

<www.rhockey.com> Roller
  Hockey Online features articles
  on gear, playing tips, pro coverage, news, and events.

CHAPTER NINE

AGGRESSIVE SKATING

DIALECT

air: Hang time when the skates are not in contact with the skating surface; also known as *getting air.*

carving: An arcing turn made across the face of a half- or quarter-pipe.

coping: The rail at the top of a half- or quarter-pipe.

drifting: A midair traverse above a half- or quarter-pipe.

dropping in: Entering a half- or quarter-pipe from above.

fakie: Rolling backward down the face of a half- or quarter-pipe; any backward movement.

flatbottom: The uncurved bottom surface of a half- or quarter-pipe.

grind plate: A replaceable, grooved, reinforced grinding surface that fits over the outside of the wheel frame; made of plastic or metal.

half-pipe: A smooth half-cylinder-shaped skating surface that flattens out at 8 to 10 feet with a wall up to 15 feet high.

invert: A handstand done on the coping before coming back down.

(continued on next page)

How do they do that!? It's impossible to watch somebody roll backward down a set of stairs, leap over a garbage can, and do a 360 before landing, or execute an inverted, twisting, skate-grabbing flip off the lip of a half-pipe, without being impressed and just a little envious. The fact that people actually think up and want to do such things is astonishing enough, but even more impressive is the amount of single-minded practice that enables a skater to finally conquer the tricks of the trade.

Although the best aggressive skaters make their tricks look easy, they're not. These athletes have built their skills starting with a foundation of curb stalls, low ramp launches, spins on flat pave-

Skating a spine ramp.

ment, and lots of hours on skates. Coolness factor aside, wear protective gear if you want to play at extreme skating. As the moves get bigger, so do the risks. "Intact skin and bones are much more comfortable than the unfortunate outcome of a forgotten set of knee pads," warns Bettina Bigelow, a California-based certified ramp instructor.

To get into aggressive skating, you need excellent balance and a solid mastery of basic turns, forward and backward skating, and stopping. For a future on the big ramps, you should also be adept at coasting in the scissors stance (see page 28). Finally, know your limits and when to back off when you find yourself tiring.

Aggressive skating tends toward short bursts of intense activity. While this form of fitness comes naturally to kids, adults entering the discipline might need to do some extra strength or interval training to extend the length of their aggressive skating sessions.

History and Organization

In the early 1980s, roller skaters began to mimic the tricks they saw being done by skateboarders. Soon after Rollerblade dazzled the world with to-

day's in-line skates, the company began organizing amateur competitions and stunt team demos to expand the sport and give their new product more exposure.

Skaters with access to quarter- and half-pipes learned to do aerial tricks and other vertical stunts, while street skaters gravitated toward the extreme by launching off anything resembling a ramp to do air stunts, riding stairs and walls, and sliding down curbs, planters, and railings on their skate frames. Thus were born the two competitive disciplines of aggressive skating known today: "vert" and "street."

As interest grew, videos and photo-intensive magazines helped aggressive skaters share the latest grinds, air tricks, and other stunts. Each year, videos such as the Hoax series hit the market to inspire skaters nationwide. Film crews travel from location to location filming the hottest skaters on the most radical terrain; then they put footage to music.

Box and *Daily Bread*, a pair of aggressive-oriented magazines launched in the early 1990s, are still motivating self-proclaimed "rollerbladers" with dramatic shots and interviews with the experts. This genre of magazines uses photos and instructional pieces to encourage new skaters. For some of the lesser-known magazines, the practice of printing the drawings and photos sent in by their readers has helped build a sense of community among upcoming young aggressive skaters. (For more on magazines, see the Aggressive Resources section at the end of this chapter.)

In 1994, the Aggressive Skaters Association (ASA) was created to standardize competitions and promote this type of skating. The ASA sanctions both amateur and professional competitions worldwide using its guidelines for safety standards and contest administration and judging. In addition, the National Inline Skate Series (NISS) presents an annual series of regional competitions.

Events

Street competitions are held in an area containing ramps and walls of various heights and a variety of boxes and rails for sliding and grinding on. Contestants skate an improvised program of jumps, spins, grabs, and grinds. Ramp or **vert** (as in "vertical air") competitions are performed on a half-pipe. Here the athletes get big air off the lip to perform a 50-second series of high-flying tricks such as grabs, flips, and inverts.

The ASA's aggressive competitions are held across North America, giving skaters a consistent format and the opportunity to compete against others of similar ability. A series of local and regional contests known as the ASA Amateur Circuit gives every budding aggressive skater a shot at going pro. Divisions include 12-and-under, Open, Expert, and Women at each of the circuit's Sectional (local) and Regional events (including seven U.S. regions plus Canada). For those who reach the Finals, the top ten street male riders, the top five vert male riders, and any winning females are given the opportunity to go pro.

After proving themselves by rising through all three amateur levels, these skaters have earned the right to participate in the ASA Pro Tour and other media-grabbing events such as the X Games and Gravity Games. The ASA Pro Tour generates 105 hours of programming each year on ESPN and espn2, which is distributed to more than 180 countries outside the United States, making it truly global. The X Games are considered the premier ESPN extreme sports property. Tapping into the same audience, NBC created the Gravity Games in 1999, which generated more than 12 hours of network coverage for its selection of extreme sports, including aggressive skating.

Gear

Protective Gear

Plan for frequent crashes, which are inevitable when you're learning street and aerial moves. Don't just "wear the gear," wear really *good* gear that has been designed by and for aggressive skaters to minimize damage on impact. Here's a shopping list in order of importance.

- full-coverage, hard-shell helmet rated for multiple impact resistance (for example, Snell's N94 or the CPSC standard described on page 14)
- thick, heavy-duty knee and elbow pads with double stitching and sleeves or wide straps to keep them firmly in place in a slide
- wrist guards or fingerless gloves with a wraparound support strap and at least one splint, utilizing padded leather or Kevlar on the palm for abrasion protection and reduced sliding on ramps
- padded shorts or girdle with all-around padding
- slip-on or strap-on shin guards
- baggy pants with reinforced knees to wear over pads

Skates

Aggressive gear can be just as technical as hockey and speed gear, designed in many cases by the skaters themselves for the rigors of street and ramp skating.

Boots: As with any skate, if you don't make comfort a priority, you're wasting your money, be-

Salomon North America

Aggressive skates.

cause pain is a major deterrent to learning. Try on only skates with a thickly padded, double-stitched boot liner. Whether it's inserted into a plastic shell or integrated as part of a soft boot, pinch the tongue or sides near the ankle area to determine thickness. You'll find that cheaper skates have thinner liners.

Plan to pay a bit extra for safety features, too. Whether you buy plastic or soft boots, aggressive skates need a sturdy cuff that is strong enough to provide added support for the ankle on high-impact landings. Some skate brands offer a special shock absorber under the ball of the foot to cushion landings. Good quality boots are constructed with recessed buckles and cuff hinges so they won't catch and cause a crash when you're tackling rails, coping, or curbs.

Better brands also feature a reinforced and well-padded toe area as well as a large "soul spot," or exposed sole on either side of the bottom of the boot where the frame is attached. Look for a frame that is attached with recessed hardware so the screws won't wear out from grinding.

Frames: The most durable frames are flat rather than sculpted and have thick, short walls designed to keep the skater close to the ground for better stability when landing. Flat frames accommodate most aftermarket grind plates, although there are plates designed for use with sculpted frames. If you'll be on half-pipes, use a skate with metal frames and grind plates; for street, plastic is preferred.

Most aggressive skaters remove the heel brake to prevent catching it on grinding surfaces.

Wheels

Aggro wheels are designed to maximize stability, durability, and slide-ability. To keep you stable and low to the ground, aggressive skates are typically mounted with wide, flat wheels no larger than 67 mm. The wheel core can be made of urethane or nylon or might be missing altogether. Generally, urethane bonds better than nylon to the wheel material, making it less likely to blow apart at a bad time. Hard wheels are slower to wear out and slip more easily during slides and grinds. On the street, use wheels with 84–90A durometer rating for better grip and shock absorption; use the harder 95A or above to more easily attain the higher speeds of vert.

Like with other types of skates, bearing quality ranges from ABEC 1 to ABEC 5. When purchasing a new pair of aggressive skates, a higher ABEC will increase the price. If you can't afford faster spinning now, you can always upgrade later.

WHEEL SETUPS

- **Standard flat:** The standard recreational wheel configuration—all four wheels are of equal size and in contact with the ground—provides good stability for stairs, jumps, and ramps but isn't useful for grinding, because there isn't a sufficient gap between the center wheels.

- **Anti-rocker:** A pair of larger wheels (for example, 65 mm) is mounted at the toe and heel, and a pair of smaller, harder wheels (45 mm) is installed in the center. This setup results in a larger gap that makes it easier to "lock" onto a railing or other grindable surface. However, because the center wheels are too small to touch the ground, the trade-offs are less stability when skating and great difficulty in turning.

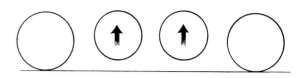

Anti-rocker setup.

- **Rockered:** Most skate frames allow you to drop the center two wheels a couple of millimeters. This "curved" blade is great for maneuverability and cornering, but because either the toe or heel wheel is off the ground at any given time, it compromises your stability and speed. A rockered setup is rarely used in aggressive skating and by only a few vert experts looking for better control on ramp transitions.

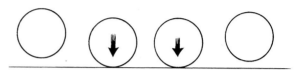

Rockered setup.

- **All small:** Skates mounted with four small, hard wheels are great for stability; the skater's center of gravity remains low, and all four wheels touch the ground during skating. This setup is also good for grinding, because the small wheels leave a fairly large gap. The trade-offs are tortoise speed and a rough, vibrating ride.

All small setup.

- **Shifted:** Vert skaters can grind without losing stability, speed, and responsiveness on the ramp by using a setup that creates a gap between the two center wheels. In a frame that accommodates it, separate the center wheels by shifting them toward the front and rear. Install slightly harder wheels in the center and keep them the same height as the others and not so hard that they slip on the ramp surface.

Shifted setup.

- **Flat rocker:** Install two center wheels that are about 3 mm smaller than the end wheels in the frame's rockered (lowered) position. Because all four wheels touch the ground when skating, this setup doesn't sacrifice speed and stability to achieve a slightly wider grinding gap.

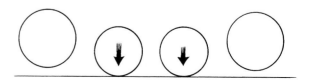

Flat rocker setup.

ROLL MODELS

The most common advice from aggressive pros is to forget about glory, fame, sponsorship, and money and simply skate for the pure joy of it. Skate hard and develop your own style—your talent will speak for itself. With enough commitment, you might even win the X Games, as did **Aaron Feinberg** on his 16th birthday in 1997, and **Arlo Eisenberg** in his early 20s. Since his X Games win, Eisenberg has become a bit of a missionary. "I have to admit winning's kind of sweet; you know, it feels good. But I certainly love rollerblading and I enjoy coming out to events like this with the [opportunity for] exposure and spreading the word. A lot of people are seeing what we do, and hopefully they'll get turned on to it. It's really a lot of fun."

If you feel the calling to teach others, act on it. **Mark Shays,** cofounder of the Aggressive Skaters Association, says, "Teaching is probably the most satisfying part of skating for me, except for the occasional day when you learn that big trick you've been working on for a long time."

Aggressive skating ICP Master Examiner **Bettina Bigelow** adds, "You really don't have to be a kid to appreciate and even enjoy aggressive skating. Just as improving your game of tennis or running that extra mile challenges your athletic ability, so will aggressive skating. You don't need to 'get air' or pull a big trick to enjoy the things that a skate park or a local street skate have to offer. You'll be amazed at how personally challenging and rewarding it is to simply roll around on a ramp. And think of how proud your kids will be when Mom goes to the skate park for the Adult Beginner Vert Class!"

Key Skills

Stopping and Speed Control

You won't be safe skating brakeless unless you can perform the stopping and speed control techniques described in chapter 2.

Directional Transitions

Transitions allow you to change direction midroll so you can switch smoothly from backward to forward motion and vice versa. The following four variations are land based. Once you've conquered these, phase out the arms as spotting aids.

FORWARD-TO-BACKWARD ROLLING TRANSITION

1. From a forward rolling coast at a moderate pace, begin a counterclockwise spin, riding the right skate while pivoting on the left toe wheel.

2. The moment the left heel wheel returns to the pavement, shift your weight onto that skate.

3. Make the right skate parallel with the left by means of a quick pivot on the right toe wheel, finishing with your weight equally balanced on both skates.

4. Complete the transition by pushing off into a backward stroke with the right skate.

BACKWARD-TO-FORWARD ROLLING TRANSITION

1. From a backward rolling coast, look over your right shoulder and at the same time push the right skate into a backward half swizzle. This shifts your weight to the left skate.

2. As your hips rotate sideways toward the direction of travel, lift and rotate the right skate until the toe is pointing toward the direction of travel; then step forward onto it.

3. Utilize the pressure still on the left skate's inside edge to push off smoothly into a forward glide on the right skate.

FORWARD-TO-BACKWARD TOE PIVOT

1. From a forward rolling coast at a moderate pace, raise both outstretched hands to shoulder height—right hand straight ahead, left hand behind—lined up with the direction of travel.

2. Scissors the right skate two inches forward.

3. With your eyes on your right hand (the leading skate corresponds to the leading arm), pivot on both skates' *toe* wheels to rotate your hips, toes, and knees counterclockwise 180 degrees.

4. Return your heels to the pavement. Your eyes and hands do not move during the entire movement. For best results, keep your knees bent and your upper body movements smooth as you rotate your lower body.

5. Learn to perform this pivot clockwise.

BACKWARD-TO-FORWARD HEEL PIVOT

1. From a backward rolling coast at a moderate pace, raise both outstretched hands to shoulder height—left hand straight ahead, right hand behind—lined up with the direction of travel. Without changing the positions of your arms, look over your shoulder at your right hand.

2. Scissors the right skate two inches backward.

3. With your eyes on your right hand (the leading skate corresponds to the leading arm), pivot on both skates' *heel* wheels to rotate your hips, toes, and knees clockwise 180 degrees.

4. Return your toes to the pavement. Your eyes and hands do not move during the entire movement. For best results, keep your knees bent and your upper body movements smooth as you rotate your lower body.

5. Learn to perform this pivot counterclockwise.

Midair Rotations

Hop turns are a trickier way to perform directional transitions. It's best to start out in your favorite direction, on a dry patch of lawn.

180-DEGREE HOP TURNS

1. On pavement, start with low 180-degree hop turns from a complete standstill, starting and ending each in a solid ready position. Be sure to hop straight up and lead your body with your head (look in the direction you plan to turn).

2. To practice at a roll, use parking space lines as spotting aids. Keeping your eyes fixed on the line, hop just high enough to rotate your hips, knees, and skates 180 degrees before making a smooth landing on flexed legs.

360-DEGREE ROTATION

1. Make a few stationary practice jumps on the lawn before trying this at a roll. Eliminate all unnecessary flailing, which can knock your center of balance out of alignment and cause a fall. The higher you leap, the more airtime you'll have to fully complete the spin before landing.

2. Make a moderate-speed approach on smooth pavement and begin coasting.

3. Position both arms to the right as you assume a prejump crouch. In one explosive movement, swing your head, arms, and hands to the left and leap up (not high), allowing your lower body to follow your upper body's twist. Lead with your head by looking over your left shoulder.

4. Keep your legs closed and arms close to the gyroscopic center of your spin to better ensure a successful landing. Flail-

ing limbs will slow your spin and can throw you off balance.

5. Spot your landing point and land in a solid ready position with both skates pointing in the direction of travel.

PRACTICE TIP

Once your 360s look good, learn to do them rolling backward (known as a Fakie 360). Use the directions above to do a backward approach, leaping twist, and landing, but pay particular attention to your feet as you launch. You'll be tempted to leap from the toes, but it's important that you push off from flat skates on all eight wheels.

Intro to Street

Increase your airtime by jumping over obstacles and launching off ramps. With each success, look for (or build) increasingly higher obstacles. Learn curb stalls in preparation for a future of curb and rail grinding.

Leap over Obstacles

1. Approach your obstacle with enough momentum to clear it. Look where you're going, not at your feet.

2. At about 5 feet out, swing both arms and use your leg and torso muscles to leap with your entire body.

3. Land with one skate slightly ahead to better distribute your balance over a longer landing platform.

PRACTICE TIP

Good form in your approach will help you keep your balance for more stable landings.

Launch Off Ramps

Start small: use speed bumps or the sides of driveways or wheelchair ramps; then work your way up.

1. Approach a driveway or wheelchair ramp at a moderate speed with knees well bent and feet in a scissors stance.

2. Spot your landing but don't look down; simply drop to it without changing your posture or flexing any muscles.

3. Land in the same flexed posture as in your approach.

Increase Air Time

1. Start trying to get extra height by going up the ramp at a crouch and extending your body just as you leave it.

2. Land in a flexed crouch and scissors your skates for maximum stability.

3. Progress to greater heights on homemade ramps (see Aggressive Resources at the end of this chapter) or on those found at skate parks.

PRACTICE TIP

You can also *reduce* the potential height of your flight by dropping your hips at the lip of the ramp to swallow the energy before extending your skates toward the pavement to land.

Conquer Curb Stalls

In the curb stall, you jump onto the edge of a curb and lock it into the space between your center wheels, pausing briefly before hopping back to the flat pavement. Develop confident curb stalls to prepare yourself for rail grinding and coping tricks on the half-pipe. The following drill is a gradual progression; you might need to repeat it for consistent success.

1. Standing still, position one skate on a curb by lodging the curb edge between

the two center wheels. Bring the other skate up next to it; then hop backward to get down before you lose your balance.

2. Facing the curb at a standstill, try hopping on with both feet and then back off.

3. To try a curb stall at a roll, skate directly toward the curb at a fairly slow speed.

4. From about a foot away, jump up and lock onto the curb with both skates.

5. Pause briefly; then hop backward to re-turn to flat pavement.

Once you are making consistently successful forward curb stalls,

○ Try a soul stall: Lock one skate onto the curb between its middle wheels and land the other skate on its outside sole (toes pointing in).

○ Start hopping back off the curb by mak-ing a 180-degree midair turn, which makes it easier to skate away from the curb for another attempt.

○ Approach from alongside the curb rather than directly facing it, so your momentum results in grinding several inches down its length.

○ Try a 180 rotation during the approach so you are landing on the curb in a backside stall.

○ Work up to 360 midair spins both in the approach and for dismounting.

○ Begin learning the same moves on rails. The safest way to try this is at your local skate park. (You can also build your own—see Aggressive Resources at the end of this chapter). Look for a rail that is only 2 to 3 inches above, and parallel to, the ground.

Street Apparatus

Skate parks offer a variety of boxes, rails, ramps, and half- or quarter-pipes to satisfy both street and

Grinding apparatus.

vert practitioners. If you're lucky enough to have one in your town, go there to work on your grind-ing and launching rather than scarring up commu-nity property. It doesn't take long to chip up a curb and alienate citizens because it's covered with shiny gray wax. Persistence in this type of activity leads to animosity toward all skaters and limita-tions on where they can skate. See Aggressive Re-sources to obtain blueprints for your own aggressive "utensils" or for information about spearheading a local skate park project.

Intro to Vert

Because many communities are building skate parks, opportunities to spend time on a half-pipe are gradually increasing. A quarter- or half-pipe allows a skater to gain enough momentum to launch high into the air and perform aerial stunts. Here are a few drills to make your first day or two on a ramp a success.

The First 10 Minutes

Spend your first moments skating in a circle on the floor of the half-pipe, also known as the flatbottom. Gradually make your way higher and higher up the transition on each side. Make the circle narrower and narrower until you're almost skating back and forth between the walls rather than circling.

Fakie

Learn to roll backward across the flatbottom. At the top of a forward roll, stay loose with your feet in a staggered narrow stance. As gravity pulls you backward, make sure you maintain the scissors stance for more stability. Stay loose as you hit the transition and ride up. When gravity stops the roll, spot the wall across the way to direct your new forward roll.

Pivot Turn

If you find the backward roll up the transition a bit harrowing, learn your 180s as soon as possible. At the top of a forward ascent, simply do a low 180-degree rotation using either a small jump or a quick toe pivot. Rotate quickly and try to fix your eyes on the middle of the ramp across the way, rather than at on your feet, to properly direct your new forward momentum.

Pumping

Learn to pump fakie-style first. Your knees draw closer to your chest during a forward ascent; take advantage of that flexed coil as you start a backward descent by pushing away from the ramp using the muscles in your thighs, hamstrings, and buttocks. As your body extends, you will feel the pump as you generate ramp-climbing energy through muscle power.

To turn and pump, at the top of a forward ascent pivot 180 degrees into a low crouch so your hips are close to the surface. As you descend, push hard to press your skates into the transition. Roll across the flatbottom and swing both arms upward to climb higher up the transition at the opposite side before your next pivot. Keep or build the momentum by repeating the quick crouching 180 followed by a deliberate push into the curved transition as you descend. Pumping this way has a feel similar to making a child's swing go higher. A long session of pumping practice can be tiring, because it makes use of the large muscles in the lower body to transfer energy into speed and higher climbs up the vert.

Deciphering Trick Names

The string of words used to name most aggressive tricks is often quite poetic. To the uninitiated, a Truespin Alley-oop Makio might sound intriguing but will be impossible to visualize. There is, however, a method to the naming based on certain core terms that allow savvy skaters to decipher individual components and envision the moves. Many aggro terms have their roots in skateboard language and are shared by snowboarders as well. Some terms have a different meaning depending on the locale of the skaters. Following are a few of the most commonly heard names for aerial and grinding tricks.

Aerial Stunts

For both street and vert, the following words describe several methods for seizing the skates while airborne, known collectively as *grabs:*

Acid drop: Performing the trick during a long drop from a high launching surface to a lower landing.

Alley-oop: A 180 rotation in the unnatural direction done either entering or exiting the stunt.

Fakie: Enter or exit the stunt traveling backward instead of forward.

Flat spin: A midair spin with the body parallel to the ground.

Japan: Reaching behind the body to grab the opposite leg while the nongrabbed leg is bent.

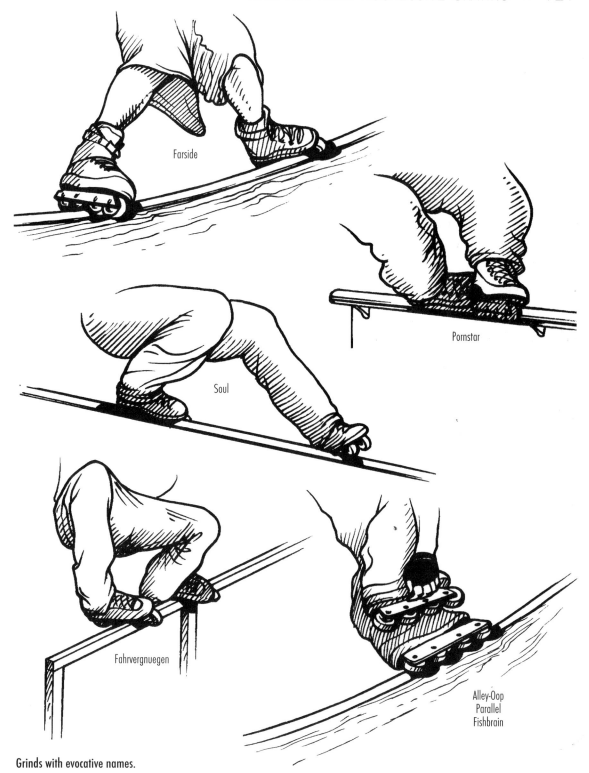

Farside

Pornstar

Soul

Fahrvergnuegen

Alley-Oop
Parallel
Fishbrain

Grinds with evocative names.

Resist grinding on city property.

Liu kang: A grab in which the nongrabbed leg kicks out as if you are doing a side kick.

Method: Grabbing the outside of the skate with the hand on the same side.

Mute: Reaching across the body to grab a skate with the hand on the opposite side.

Running man: When the legs begin to bicycle upon loss of control before a fall; also known as *air kedidi*.

Stale: Grabbing the wheels.

Besides the basic front and back **flips**, other common flips include

Brainless: A backward flip with a half spin.

Miller: A back flip in which the hand is planted midway on the coping.

Misty: A spinning flip.

Grinding Stunts

These terms describe the various foot positions involved in grinding.

Backside: A grind in which the skater mounts the curb from the side with a 90-degree counterclockwise rotation.

Fahrvergnuegen: A frontside grind entered with a 180 rotation in the unnatural direction (alley-oop) and landed on the outside sole edge of the front skate and inside sole edge of the trailing skate.

Farside: A grind performed after the skate(s) land on the far side of a rail rather than the near side.

Frontside: A grind in which the skater mounts the curb from the side with a 90-degree *clockwise* rotation.

Royale: A grind done on the inside sole edge of the front skate and on the outside sole edge of the trailing skate.

Soul: A grind in which the front skate is across the curb and the back skate is slipping down on the outside half of its sole, parallel to the curb.

AGGRESSIVE RESOURCES

ORGANIZATIONS

Aggressive Skaters Association
(ASA)
13468 Beach Ave.
Marina del Rey CA 90292
Todd Shays, Executive Director
310-823-1865
fax 310-823-4146
E-mail: asa@asaskate.com
www.ASAskate.com
The ASA is a membership association that produces more than 100 professional and amateur events each year in more than 20 countries.

National Inline Skate Series
(NISS)
c/o Anywhere Sports Productions
7875 Hillside Ave.
Hollywood CA 90046
Mark Billik, Director
323-851-3770
fax 323-851-3710
E-mail: msbillik@fea.net
www.agrosk8.com/home.html
Annual series of competitive events for amateur skaters and professionals vying for the NISS U.S. Championship crown. The International Inline Skate Series (IISS) puts on associated international-level competitions.

IISA Government Relations
Committee
201 N. Front St. #306
Wilmington NC 28401
Dave Cooper, Director
313-942-323

E-mail: iisagr@aol.com
www.iisa.org
Protects skater access rights nationwide.

CAMPS

Camp Woodward
Box 93, Route 45
Woodward PA 16882
814-349-5633
fax 814-349-5643
E-mail: office@woodwardcamp.
com
www.woodwardcamp.com/
inline.htm
Instruction on bowls, miniramps, vert ramps, rails, and street; grind rails made to pro specifications.

E-ZINES

817 Mag, <www.817mag.net>
ASA, <www.ASAskate.com>
Be-Magazine, <www.be-mag.
com>
FBI skaters, <www.fbiskaters.com>
Sequence, <www.sequencemag.
com>
Scum Magazine, <www.
scummagazine.com>
Skeptic Industries, <www.
skepticindustries.com>
WASN, <www.xtremecentral.
com/bladegrl/>

PUBLICATIONS

*Inline! A Manual of Intermediate
to Advanced Technique.*
William Nealy. Birmingham AL:
Menasha Ridge Press, 1998.
Box Magazine

Chris Mitchell, Publisher
Petersen Publishing Co.
6420 Wilshire Blvd.
Los Angeles CA 90048-5515
800-627-6157
Daily Bread Magazine
Angie Walton, Editor
P.O. Box 82146
San Diego CA 92138-2146
619-744-0848

RAMP AND RAIL SUPPLIERS

American Ramp Company
1106 N. Webb
Webb City MO 64870
877-726-7778
fax 417-673-0324
E-mail: arc@sofnet.com
www.arc-ramp.com/about_us.html
Designs and builds ramps and skate parks.

Hot Rails, Inc.
45 Park Place S., Suite 101
Morristown NJ 07960
973-283-2631
fax 973-283-2632
E-mail: sales@hotrails.com
www.hotrails.com/ramp.htm
Provides ready-made ramps.

Rollersparks, Inc.
322 W. 106th St.
New York NY 10025
800-772-7539
fax 212-665-0905
Blueprints for ramps and half-pipes.
(continued on next page)

AGGRESSIVE RESOURCES *(continued from previous page)*

RECOMMENDED MANUFACTURERS

Bulletproof (protective gear): 714-650-7769

Crash Pads (padded shorts): 800-964-5993, <www.crash-pads.com>

Harbinger (protective gear): 800-729-5954, <www.harbingersports.com>

Mosa Extreme Sports (Pro-Tec helmets): 310-318-9883, <www.mosa.com> (under construction)

Tribe Distribution (Senate gear, apparel): 714-375-4101

Triple Eight (protective gear): 212-681-6244, <www.triple8.com>

WEBSITES

<www.aggressive.com> Justin Anderson's Aggressive.com is the most informative and easy to read site for entry-level and advanced aggro skaters. He includes grind rail building instructions, photographs, online magazines, video clips, tutorials for street and ramp skills, a list of skate parks, treatments for common injuries—even snippets of creative writing!

<www.bayinsider.com/partners/heckler> Heckler Magazine's ramp plans website has specifications and diagrams for building your own fun box, pyramid, launch ramp, and half- and quarter-pipes.

<www.iisa.org/skatepark> The IISA's Skate Park Startup Guide is where to go for information about getting your own skate park built.

<www.asaskate.com/wasn> The Women's Aggressive Skating Network is part of the Aggressive Skating Association and strives to make its events as fun for female competitors as for males. Special judging rules allow women to advance up the Amateur Circuit regardless of low numbers in female participation.

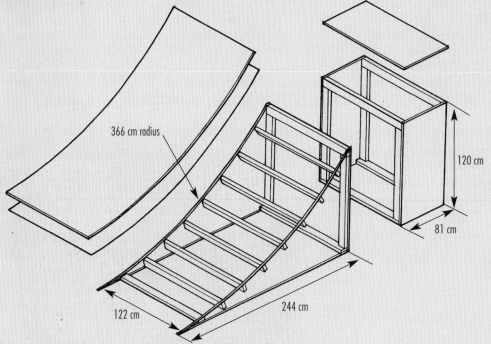

366 cm radius

120 cm

81 cm

122 cm

244 cm

Plans for a launch ramp, quarter pipe detail. (Courtesy *Heckler Magazine*)

■ CHAPTER TEN ■

TECHNICAL DOWNHILL

DIALECT

angulation: The angle of the body to the ground, dictated by the degree of tipping at the knee, waist, or—in a fast, banked turn—the whole body.

gates: Hinged, "breakaway" posts fixed to weighted bases; used to mark in-line slalom courses.

jump turns: An advanced stopping method utilizing a series of hopping turns to keep corresponding edges across the fall line.

over rotation: Twisting the upper body to change the edge set.

snowplow: A wide, forward swizzle that utilizes hip muscles and edges to increase friction in order to slow down and eventually stop.

As soon as he entered Oltmans' draft Merkert stood up and gave his legs a drink of blood. Standing in a loose crouch with poles in front of face, like an Alpine Super G racer might do for some moderate twistys, left Merkert still over-taking Oltmans quickly—too quickly. Merkert stood up higher to slow down. Some sticky tar grabbed Merkert's left StreetSki, pulled it backward and twisted his body to the left. Terror ruled. An emergency move to a lower, more stable body position allowed Merkert to regain his balance but, again, caused him to gain ground too quickly on Oltmans.

—*Excerpt from* The Zolar Mammoth Downhill Festival Race Report, 1999 *by George Merkert.*

In-line disciples of descent compete by either harnessing speed or increasing it. If you have the skills of a ski racer and the mental fortitude of a downhiller, this sport is for you. Of course, you

Doug Lucht

Douglas Lucht sets an in-line downhill world record at 63 miles per hour.

should be a gold-tassel graduate of chapters 2 and 5 before even considering this skating discipline. Here's your starting gun!

History

Francois Hyacinthe was the first to wear full leathers and a downhill ski helmet; in his early 1990s' speed record attempts he even attached aerodynamic fins to his calves. In 1998 Douglas Lucht was recorded going 63 miles per hour on his own invention, extended frame StreetSkis. Patrick Naylor, an exquisitely prepared 39-year-old, won the 1998 X Games downhill event, capitalizing on race strategy and gear-based aerodynamics. ESPN's broad coverage of the games brought an untamed version of in-line downhill to the attention of Americans everywhere.

Over the years, downhill experts have honed and shared their techniques. Californians Steve MacDonald, Todd Ray, and Scott Peer have contributed not only to this chapter but also to the growth of skater and media interest, downhill and slalom techniques, and competitive opportunities. Inaugurated by their grassroots efforts, regional training sessions and contests are now regularly scheduled in areas where interest is high.

Todd Ray, author of the *Ultimate Skating Guide to the San Francisco Bay Area*, first coined the term *technical downhill*. It's an appropriate moniker for the slalom disciplines, because control on steep asphalt pitches requires precise and subtle kinetic movements that, as with its alpine predecessor, require dedicated practice to master.

Events

There is no official governing body for in-line downhill competitions. Various groups organize races and speed record attempts. These include promoters of luge/bobsled, skateboard, and multisport events, regional clubs, and area retailers. (See the list of promoters in the Downhill Resources section at the end of this chapter.) With no official standards or guidelines, events follow whatever format the organizer chooses.

The Westwood Ski and Sports Club in southern California is the source of most of the training and competitive activity on the West Coast, perhaps the most in the United States.

Slalom Races

In-line downhill competitions usually offer slalom and giant slalom races on courses defined with cones or weighted, breakaway gates. Except on the cone slalom courses, they normally produce speeds from 25 to 35 miles per hour. The cones or gate configurations determine the various courses. Ski poles are optional.

A large field of competitors is reduced through preliminary heats, either by counting the fastest of two or three runs or based on the combined total times of each athlete's heats.

- **Slalom with cones:** Technical courses are prepared with cones lined up 1 or 2 meters apart, resulting in tight offset turns and higher speeds. Competitors use ski-style slalom techniques similar to alpine skiing or snowboarding.

- **Skates-and-gates slalom:** This race is run on a course with gates (hinged poles about 5 feet tall). Racers slap the gates briefly to the pavement, passing as close as possible to find the shortest route. Speeds reach up to 25 miles per hour.

- **Giant slalom:** A giant slalom course dictates technically challenging high-speed descents. These courses are longer than the skates-and-gates runs but also feature hinged gates. GS racers often reach 35 miles per hour.

- **Super G:** Think "super giant slalom" and you've got the picture.

Downhill Races

Any race billed as a downhill is guaranteed to be terrifyingly fast. It's unfortunate that the only downhill in-line racing most U.S. citizens have seen is the pack-style races on ESPN's X Games in the late 1990s. Although many legitimately qualified racers participated, the media exposure and prize money attracted other competitors with more guts than skill. Short on safety standards, the event's thrills and spills painted a death-defying picture. Downhill was removed from the X Games after Patrick Naylor's win in 1998.

There is plenty of downhill action overseas. Each year a full season of races attracts large audiences in France, Italy, Germany, Belgium, Austria, and Switzerland. In Europe there are two types of downhill events: courses set up on winding mountain roads and harrowing races down existing bobsled courses.

The mountain courses are 3 kilometers in length and have a mass start. The biggest of these races is held in Lausanne, Switzerland, attracting over 300 participants. The final field is screened through two rounds of qualification runs. Audiences reach up to 100,000.

The typical bobsled run features serpentine, nonstop downgrades and a narrow half-pipe whose surface is heavily textured (the better to retain ice in winter). This makes bobsled downhills wild and fast. Once a competitor enters the course there is no way to bail out, and T-stops are next to useless because the tight radius of the rough, curved surface prevents a solid five-wheel drag.

Geared for downhill speed on StreetSkis.

Gear

Gravity-fueled velocity increases your chances for injury; crashes here result in long downhill slides, threatening deep abrasions or a fractured hand, forearm, or shoulder bone. Even so, injury statistics for events put on by race promoters with established safety standards are on the decline, thanks to improved skill levels and new technologies that minimize road rash and skeletal damage.

Skates

Most racers compete on five-wheel speed skates; a few use long, six-wheel, flexible frame skates (StreetSki or Rossignol brands) equipped with standard alpine ski bindings for use with ski boots. Like other in-line racers, all competitors use fast bearings and wheels selected for optimum performance on the race course's surface.

Brakes

Heel brakes and adapters for five-wheel racing skates usually must be special ordered because they are not standard equipment. When not available from the manufacturer, they must be custom built and installed.

Protective Gear

Knee pads must be sturdy and able to stay firmly in place. For the best protection, use the heavier pads aggressive skaters wear.

Hip pads reduce the possibility of a fractured pelvis or coccyx. Bike shorts with tailbone and hip pads fit underneath a looser pair of shorts or pants. Heavier-duty brands feature thick exterior ribbed

ROLL MODEL

In the 1980s I tried roller skates, but I was not impressed with them, and stuck with my bicycle. But then around 1990 a friend of mine got a pair of Rollerblades and invited me to try them on an in-line skates-and-gates slalom course. I was instantly hooked. After a couple of years running gates in low-traffic streets, we got a permit at West L.A. College and started training and organizing races there.

I started getting progressively better skates and going faster. Besides slalom, downhill tuck runs and speedskating became regular parts of my skating. In 1997 I talked my way into a wildcard invitation to the ESPN X Games. In the first round I caught Eddy Matzger and Dan Burger playing too much strategy and sprinted into the second round. In that round Chad Smith blasted out of the start, setting a blazing pace, and he and Pat Naylor (the 1998 champ) ultimately eliminated me.

Each season is full of surprises, which is one of the things that keep me interested. But the main reasons I race are the camaraderie and the sheer thrill.

—Scott Peer, world-class downhill competitor and southern California clinic instructor

padding. Other options include baseball sliding shorts or hip pads designed for roller hockey or aggressive skating.

To participate in downhill events, competitors are usually required to wear full body suits. Leather, Kevlar, and the SkidSkins line (see Downhill Resources at the end of this chapter) offer abrasion protection and light padding, while a rubber or Lycra downhill ski suit over the top reduces wind drag.

Your hands need "industrial strength" protection. Competitions require leather gloves; some competitors use full-weight hockey gloves

to protect against abrasions and wrist and thumb injuries.

Some races require a **full-face helmet** with a rigid chin guard. Downhillers often choose aerodynamic speed helmets like those alpine downhill skiers use. For training, use your ski helmet, if you own one, or an aggressive skating helmet. These offer better head coverage than a bike or skating helmet (see page 113).

Other Downhill Gear

Ski poles are optional for skates-and-gates and downhill races. See the skate-to-ski Gear section, page 66, for details about the adjustable-length Leki brand and how to prepare pole tips for use on pavement.

Cones are useful for training in preparation for gates. Buy a dozen or two that are heavy enough to not blow away.

Key Skills

Basic Technique

Because it is very dangerous for skaters lacking proficiency in speed control and stopping, don't attempt to learn any of the techniques described in this section unless you have mastered all of the Hill

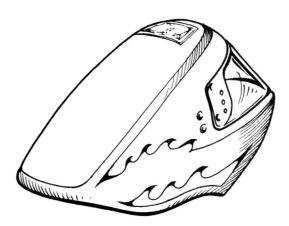

Speed helmet.

Skills described on page 28 and the basic technique of slalom turns described on page 68.

Slowing Down and Stopping

Even when fast times are the primary goal, finishing a course brakeless, approaching a tight turn, or the impending loss of control on the steeps are all good reasons to learn how to reduce your speed in ways other than using a heel brake. (However, for this type of skating, a heel brake is strongly advised!)

SLOWING SLALOMS

The best way to reduce speed without braking is a hard-cutting series of ski-style slaloms across the fall line that utilizes both skates' wheel edges to create friction. Unlike the flowing, speed-loving turns you normally use, this type of slalom incorporates a quick and dynamic scissoring action to maximize edging and friction.

At the moment of greatest pressure on the downhill, carving skate,

1. Without extending your body, release the pressure on both skates and shift both heels laterally across the hill while your skates rotate slightly toward the new turn direction. (See Lateral Hop Turns on page 70). Stay in a compressed stance to attain the angulation necessary for a deep edge set going into the new turn.

2. Scissors the new uphill skate to the front scissors position, tipped onto its outside wheel edges. Both sets of wheel edges carve across the hill to reduce your speed. Rotate your torso slightly toward the turn and keep your center of gravity behind both sets of edges to compound the pressure.

3. Immediately before starting the next turn, close the staggered stance by letting the downhill skate catch up to the uphill one.

4. Shift your weight onto the uphill skate and initiate a new turn.

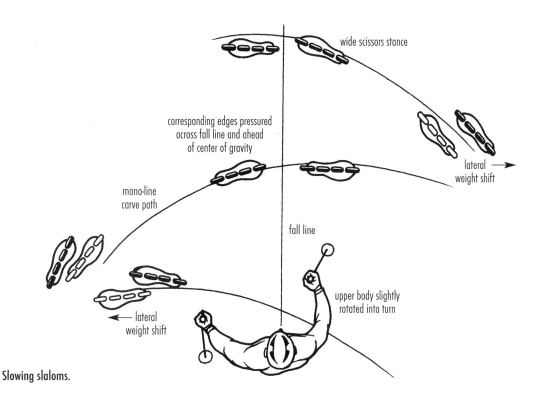

Slowing slaloms.

HOW TO SAVE YOUR SKIN

Try these tips from Scott Peer.

- **Test drive a new course:** At first, enter the gates near the bottom of the course to prevent unmanageable speed buildup; then work your way higher as you master the lower gates.
- **Roll with the crunch:** Get out of the habit of breaking a fall with your hands. Instead, develop an instinctive rolling tumble so you're less likely to break a hand, arm, or shoulder on impact with the pavement.
- **Wear heavy armor** so you can relax and skate more aggressively, stay focused, and just have more fun. Even pro downhill racers wear it—that's how we stay healthy long enough to get fast.
- **Reduce your chances of crashing** by increasing the traction from your skate components:
  - Use softer wheels: for example, 78A durometer instead of 82A.
  - Use new wheels, which have better traction and are more stable than worn wheels.
  - Stock up on brake pads. The traction from a good heel brake can help you escape many high-speed close calls.
  - Use five-wheel skates, which have better traction and stability than four-wheelers.

—Scott Peer, excerpted from "When Gear Meets the Ultimate Text," Get Rolling Orbit Online Newsletter, spring 1998

Here are some key points to remember when drilling.

- Distribute your weight evenly over the staggered skates for better stability. A narrow stance, where the rear, downhill skate nearly traces the same path as the lead skate, makes it easier to steer them across and, if necessary, up the hill to cut short your run.

- Make fast-tempo turns to keep your edges pointed across—rather than down—the fall line, connected by the fast, scissoring swap from one set of uphill edges to the other.

- Practice keeping your lower body well flexed (hips close to the pavement) so you can take advantage of the increased angulation potential to tip the skates on edge more quickly and easily.

- Keep both ankles loose and relaxed inside your boots so you can easily roll them to the sides and increase the depth of your edge set.

- Keep your body uphill from your tilted edges when they're slicing across the fall line. This enables your weight to compound the pressure and friction.

OVERROTATION

No matter how steep the hill, there is a brief moment in each carve when your body is in a neutral position from which it's easy to turn your skates slightly uphill to prevent unwanted acceleration. Timing is everything: If you rotate too soon, your skates will skid because you're still moving too fast. Rotate too late, and you'll gain speed. This technique is best learned with the help of a pair of poles.

1. Finish a slalom turn by rotating your upper body away from the fall line so that your shoulders, hips, knees, and skates are facing across the hill, rather than down it. (But keep the uphill hand in sight.)

2. Reach downhill and plant the pole to initiate a new turn.

3. Begin the new carve and untwist so that shoulders, hips, knees, and skates are all

momentarily traveling in the same direction.

4. Finish this turn with your shoulders rotated away from the fall line, now facing the opposite side of the hill.

To force a stop while doing this, you would simply continue rotating the upper body uphill and skip the pole plant. Your skates will carve a tight arc and end up pointing uphill, terminating downhill progress.

OTHER SLOWING AND STOPPING TECHNIQUES

A few daring experts have learned how to slow and stop using a series of aggressive jump turns that resembles a fast alpine skiing stop. For normal mortals, a variety of techniques are covered in the Speed Control section starting on page 30, where you can review instructions for a T-stop, snowplow, and the safest ways to bail out.

Racing Strategies

Obviously, downhill racers want to go faster, not slower. If you are brave enough to toss aside all your speed-reduction techniques, here is a compilation of the most common high-speed advice offered by today's experts.

- **Aerodynamics:** A rubber suit and a speed helmet can shave off valuable seconds. To improve stability and reduce skate wobble in your tuck, keep a wide stance with your weight evenly distributed between right and left skates and shifted slightly toward the back wheels.

- **Edgeless skating:** The farther you tip your skates onto the wheel edges, the more friction they create and the more they slow you down. Remember, edging is the key to *reducing* speed.

- **Endurance:** Downhill racers must be strong enough to maintain a deep tuck for the entire descent. Condition yourself with fitness skating and resistance training at the gym (see chapter 3).

- **Know the course:** For better confidence, make several practice runs to introduce yourself to a new course, look for escape routes, and plan cornering strategy.

- **Pack experience:** In mass-start races, your ability to win might ride solely on your knowledge of how to capitalize on fellow competitors' weaknesses, drafting and pack strategies, and other race tactics. See speed skating pack tips beginning on page 97.

- **Skiing through gates:** Using the forearm of the arm toward the center of the course to hit the gates is called an inside clear. The more efficient method is an outside clear; here the forearm facing away from the course is used, allowing the racer to cut a tighter, faster line. Both methods require precise timing.

Downhill Resources

Event Promoters and Sanctioning Groups

Alternative International Sports
   (AIS)
9393 N. 90th St., Suite 102-249
Scottsdale AZ 85258
602-677-9511

Federation of International Gravity
   Racers (FIGR)
949-722-1800, ext. 26
E-mail: beausk8@aol.com

Gravity Games
The Gravity Games series (including aggressive and downhill in-line competitions) are festivals of alternative sports, lifestyles, and music, sponsored by NBC Sports Ventures.
The Arcade
65 Weybosset St., Suite 60
Providence RI 02903
877-7-GRAVTY/877-747-2889
   or 401-621-3150
www.gravitygames.com/
   index_home.cfm

Extreme Downhill International
   (EDI)
Biker Sherlock
1666 Garnet Ave., #308
San Diego CA

619-272-3095
fax 619-272-3097
E-mail: biker@dregsskateboards.
   com
www.dregsskateboards.com/
   gravity.html

In-Line Slalom Skaters International
   (ISSI)
Pete Beatty, President
28 Paragon Ln.
Stamford CT 06905
203-357-0225 or 888-SK8-
   WORKS/888-758-9675
In development; an organizing body intended to govern in-line ski, speed, and freestyle slalom competitions.

Products

StreetSki
Douglas Lucht
16524 E. Laser Dr., Suite 2
Fountain Hills AZ 85268
480-816-8200
fax 480-816-8638
E-mail: streetski@extremezone.com
www.streetski.com

SkidSkins
Lamarjean Group, Inc.,
   SkidSkins Division
16776 Bernardo Center Dr.
Suite 110-B PMB 179

San Diego CA 92128
888-590-6800
   or 858-674-6519
fax 858-675-9251
E-mail: jake@skidskins.com
www.skidskins.com

Leki
LEKI USA, Inc.
356 Sonwil Dr.
Buffalo NY 14225
800-255-9982 or 716-683-1022
E-mail: service@leki.com
www.leki.com

Poly Enterprises, Inc.
230 E Pomona Ave.
Monrovia CA 91016
626-358-5116
fax 626-358-7862
www.polyenterprises.com

Websites

<www.members.aol.com/
   wwskiclub/inline.htm> Westwood Ski and Sports Club lists skate-to-ski training and competition events; clinic organizer Scott Peer's home base.
<www.getrolling.com/orbit/
   techDownhill.html> 1997 Get Rolling ORBIT article, "Technical Downhill," by Steve MacDonald.

Anibal Garcia by Heather Harding

CHAPTER ELEVEN

HYBRID TEAM SPORTS

DIALECT

free kick-in: After a halt by the referee, returning the ball to play by kicking it from the designated spot (at least 10 feet from the goal zone).

goal crease: A semicircle arcing from the center of the goal line. Also known as the *goal zone.*

goal intrusion violation: Called when an offensive player enters the opponent's goal zone in an obstructive or potentially harmful manner.

goaltending violation: Called when two or more players are inside their own goal zone during a potential scoring situation.

handball violation: Called when the ball contacts a player's hand or arm. (It's not a violation if the hands were protecting the player's face or torso.)

major penalty kick-in: A two-person, 3-second play that returns the ball to play after a major penalty, such as checking or roughness.

(continued on next page)

What happens when you combine one part creative thinking with one part sport devotion and roll them out on a smooth surface? A new in-line team sport, that's what. Fortunately, narrow-minded doubters and disbelievers did not sidetrack the committed athletes who shaped the rules that define today's roller soccer and roller basketball games. And with the growing ranks of youngsters who spent their childhood on skates, not only will these sports continue to grow, but new ones are likely to sprout.

ROLLER SOCCER

Roller soccer is a unique and fast-moving game that capitalizes on a skater's agility, balance, and finesse. This hybrid team sport combines in-line skating with modified rules borrowed from soccer. Because it discourages rough physical contact and rewards skill and fair team play, roller soccer appeals to boys, girls, men, and women of all sizes and ages. Skaters from all disciplines find that roller soccer improves their quickness and balance for other sports.

The following information has been compiled from excerpts of The Official Rollersoccer International Federation website at <*www.rollersoccer.com*>, thanks to the cooperation of founder and president Zack Phillips.

History and Organization

Roller soccer was born in San Francisco's Golden Gate Park, a location cherished by skaters long before in-lines were invented. Because several streets here are closed to automobile traffic every Sunday, one group of friends took to kicking and passing a pinecone up the road. In December 1995, it occurred to Zack

DIALECT (continued from previous page)

One member of the nonpenalized team kicks the ball into play from a location no more than 20 feet from his or her goal, while the penalized player tries to defend from a position between that location and the goal. After 3 seconds, play is halted, the penalized player is removed, and play is resumed with a free kick-in.

minor penalty kick-in: A play that returns the ball to play after a minor penalty, such as offsides skating. A member of the nonpenalized team kicks the ball back into play from a spot near where it exited the pitch.

penalty box: A rinkside bench where violating players sit out of play to serve penalty time.

pitch: The playing surface or court.

power play: A team configuration that occurs when one team has more players on the pitch than the other team due to a player serving penalty time in the penalty box. The penalized team is limited to a maximum of four players on the pitch while penalty time is being served.

throw-in: Returning the ball to play (after it crosses outside the rink) by tossing it in within 5 seconds of hand contact; done by a member of the team opposite the one whose player last touched the ball.

Phillips to bring a soccer ball to the park. The skaters proceeded to mark off a playing area, and within moments the diverse group was enthusiastically participating in the first roller soccer match.

When an expanse of asphalt at San Francisco's North Beach Playground became available, regular Wednesday night games began to attract even more new roller soccer players. By November 1996, the playground hosted weekly scheduled matches, while other games took place in Golden Gate Park and a local indoor roller hockey facility.

Zack Phillips's passion for roller soccer led him to create Rollersoccer International Federation (RSIF), the governing body over which he presides. League members play at a local RSIF-affiliated rink. RSIF membership guarantees that matches follow a standard structure and provide players with a supervised opportunity to improve skills and teamwork. By the late 1990s, RSIF was governing indoor roller soccer leagues in ten American cities and nine countries.

Today, RSIF schedules its season of events across the country with a series of exhibition games and roller soccer tournaments. In 1999, the organization offered Skate, Dribble, and Shoot! (SDS) skills contests in conjunction with the Diversity Tour (a series of skate festivals featuring aggressive skating competitions). These contests provided a fun and challenging way to get more skaters involved in the growing sport.

Zack Phillips

Roller soccer attracts all ages.

Rules

Complete and official roller soccer rules are detailed on the RSIF website at <*www.rollersoccer. com/rules/complete_rules.html*>. The following overview will get you started.

Rink Specifications

Contact RSIF to find your closest roller rink affiliate. League court or "pitch" dimensions are 200 by 85 feet (60 by 26 m). If space is limited, a smaller pitch of 180 by 70 feet (55 by 21 m) is allowed. A penalty box and player benches are positioned along the perimeter close to the midfield stripe. Outdoor games are played on a tennis or roller hockey court or other smooth, flat surface with boards around the perimeters.

A midfield strip bisects the width of the pitch; at its exact center is the kick-off spot. Twelve-foot goal lines are centered 10 feet from each end of the pitch, and a 6-foot-radius semicircle marks the goal zone at the center of each goal line.

The Game

In league matches, five-player teams play two 25 minute periods, with a 5-minute halftime break. The clock stops for injuries, major penalties, and official time-outs; during the last 2 minutes of each half it stops for minor penalties as well. If a match is tied after 50 minutes of play, a two-on-two tiebreaker (with no team member substitutions allowed) determines the winner. Unlimited team member substitutions are allowed during regular play.

A kick-off by the visiting team starts the action at the beginning of each half, with all defending team members at least 10 feet away from the kick-off point. The ball also comes into play through goal kicks, throw-ins, and kick-ins. Players advance the ball with their feet, body, or head. Defenders skate alongside or backward ahead of offensive players and try to steal the ball away. After a goal is scored, the nonscoring team clears the ball from the goal cage and the game continues uninterrupted.

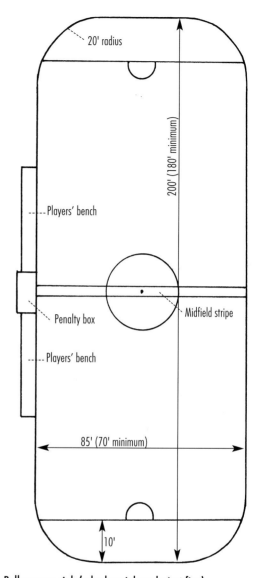

Roller soccer rink (a hockey rink works just fine).

Members of the scoring team cannot defend until the ball has been advanced across the midfield stripe. Team members, including the goaltender, are not allowed to use their hands to move the ball. As a result, there is no regulated goaltender position, meaning that all team members defend their goal.

Only one defensive player and one offensive player are allowed in the marked goal zone, or

Roll Model

My son Keeton, 11 at the time he learned about roller soccer, was already an avid skater and a great soccer player. He was so excited—here was a game that joined his two favorite sports. I was a bit dubious at first; I didn't want him participating in extreme sports. But when I checked out the Rollersoccer website, this appeared to be a safe team game.

From a parent's perspective, Keeton's involvement with roller soccer has been great. He plays in a league on Wednesday evenings and at the pickup games in Golden Gate Park on Sundays. As a member of the official RSIF SkateBallers Squad, he has participated in exhibition games in Pasadena at the Major League Soccer Final and at many other sports events around California. He has enjoyed the team-building experience of being involved in a new sport and is learning that he is a great skater.

The rules of roller soccer, although few, focus on safety and no bodily contact. Kids, adults, males, and females all play together, because the game is about finesse and excellence, not brute strength. I like that.

—Peter Marcus, proud dad and Director of Marketing, Rollersoccer International Federation

crease, during potential scoring opportunities. The ball is out of play when it enters the goal cage, it crosses outside the rink's perimeter, or the referee stops the game. If the ball goes outside the rink, it is thrown in from the exit point. When a referee has stopped the game, the ball is kicked back into play from a location the referee designates.

Scoring and Penalties

The team in control of the ball earns 1 point by kicking it across the goal line and into the goal cage. If the ball passes between the legs of a defender on its path into the goal, it's a 2-point score. If the score occurs while the opposing team has two or more players in the penalty box, the scoring team earns an additional bonus point.

Minor penalties include maneuvering the ball with the hands, delaying the game, skating offside (more than three players on either half of the rink at the same time), minor misconduct, and dangerous play. Major penalties are using the hand to interfere with a goal shot, major misconduct, taunting a referee, or accumulating three minor penalties. These are paid off with a penalty kick plus a 2-minute time penalty. Players who incur two major penalties must leave the game, and the team suffers a penalty kick.

Gear

Standard recreational skates work fine for roller soccer. Both in-line and conventional skates are approved for league matches. All players must wear helmets. Team members (up to 10 are allowed) must wear matching jerseys. Protective pads—gloves, wrist guards, elbow and knee pads, shin guards, and padded shorts—are strongly recommended but not required.

For league play, a goal cage consisting of a netted support frame 1 meter high by 3 meters wide is required. RSIF recommends the sturdy inflatable goals manufactured by Sportogo, because they enhance player safety. Cones or smaller goals are acceptable for local leagues or informal matches. Roller soccer uses a standard, size-5 soccer ball.

Key Skills

The best roller soccer players have or develop excellent one-footed balance for ball handling and are able to make quick starts, stops, and turns with great agility. The other skills used in playing the game are

Cut: Making a quick change of direction while advancing with the ball.

Instep kick: A kick made with the top inside part of the foot. Once learned, this fairly difficult kick results in the most powerful and accurate shooting and assists. On smooth playing surfaces it can cause a curve ball.

Side kick: A kick made with the middle of the wheel frame on the inside of the foot; used for shooting accuracy and ball control when passing or advancing.

Toe kick: A kick made with the tip of the skate (boot toe or toe wheel). Light toe kicks are used for advancing the ball. More forceful toe kicks are used for close-range shooting.

ROLLER BASKETBALL

Basketball enthusiasts who have had to quit playing their favorite game due to knee problems will love taking up roller basketball, a blend of in-line skating with one of America's other favorite sports. It attracts not only avid basketball players but also hockey players and other skaters ready for a change. In fact, the game is a safe form of team recreation for all. On a properly cleaned court there are no hills to cause unwanted acceleration; there are no manhole covers, curbs, wet leaves, or pebbles to trip you and cause injury; there are no cars, cyclists, or pedestrians to worry about. Women players can hold their own against men; in roller basketball, strength and position are not nearly as important as speed and movement without the ball.

The following information has been compiled from excerpts of the Roller Basketball website at <*www.nibbl.com*>, thanks to the cooperation of National Inline Basketball League (NIBBL) founder and commissioner Tom LaGarde.

History and Organization

The first roller basketball team was born in the fall of 1992 with an announcement in the New York Road Skaters Association (NYRSA) newsletter. Starting as a full-court two-on-two game, play

ROLLER SOCCER RESOURCES

Rollersoccer International
  Federation
P.O. Box 423318
San Francisco CA 94142-3318
888-475-7727
fax 415-437-0859
E-mail: RSIF@rollersoccer.com
www.rollersoccer.com
Zack Phillips, Founder and President;
Peter Marcus, Director of Marketing;
Dan Craddock, Director of Affiliate Programs and Membership

Tom LaGarde

A rolling jump shot.

DIALECT

2-point shot: A shot made from inside an arc 19 feet from the basket.

3-point shot: A shot made from between arcs 19 and 25 feet from the basket.

4-point shot: A shot made from outside an arc 25 feet from the basket.

body checking: A hockey-style bodily impact violation; results in ejection from the game.

field goal: Any 2-, 3-, or 4-point shot.

out-of-bounds: A violation where both skates and the ball are outside the court's marked perimeter. One skate and the ball can both be outside the line without violation as long as the other skate is touching or within the line.

traveling: A violation in which the player possessing the ball starts stroking to accelerate without dribbling at the same time. A 10-foot glide is the maximum allowed with the ball in hand, either upon gaining possession of the ball or after picking up one's dribble.

evolved to three-on-three and eventually to four players on each team, with skate-specific rules honed during every game. The National Inline Basketball League (NIBBL) formed in 1994 with the first organized games in New York City. That same year, NIBBL began playing exhibition games at NBA and in-line expositions.

Throughout the 1995 season the NIBBL All Stars played a 15-city roller basketball tour sponsored by Gatorade to showcase the sport in 30-minute exhibition games held during Gatorade's Hoop-It-Up tournaments. About the same time, the sport went international with the formation of Portugal's Organização Inline Basquetebol de Setubal, and DRIBBL, the Dutch Roller and Inline Basketball League in the Netherlands. As the 1900s drew to a close, a German league was germinating in Berlin.

The first NIBBL World Championships capped off the 1994 season. In July 1996, the Junior Inline Basketball League (JIBBL) was formed. Today, all play in both leagues begins in May and finishes with the World Championships each October. As of 1999 there were ten active New York area teams with the sport beginning to spread across the United States.

The National Inline Basketball League was founded by Tom LaGarde, a 6'10" (7'2" on skates) ex-pro basketball player who after five knee operations could no longer tolerate the pain that resulted

from playing on foot. With an NBA championship ring and a 1976 Olympic gold medal for basketball, he wasn't willing to give up his favorite sport without a fight. A pair of in-lines was the answer.

NIBBL governs roller basketball leagues and offers leadership and guidance to participants both in and outside the United States. Currently there are four in-line basketball leagues in the United States.

- National Inline Basketball League (NIBBL)
- Junior Inline Basketball League (JIBBL) (13- to 15-year-olds)
- Senior JIBBL (16- to 18-year-olds)
- Junior JIBBL (under 13)

NIBBL's USA National team travels overseas to play against teams in Portugal, France, and the Netherlands. In 1999, a special stunt team known as the NIBBL Globe Rollers promoted the sport by playing exhibition games made more exciting by the addition of ramps and dunks.

Rules

Complete and official roller basketball rules are detailed on the NIBBL website at <*www.nibbl.com/nibbl/game/rules.html*>. The following overview will get you started.

ROLL MODEL

If you are already an accomplished basketball player and a very good skater, you can be one of the best roller basketball players in the world. Anyone with good skating skills will have an immediate advantage over someone who can't skate as well but knows how to play basketball. But over time, the player who knows basketball and then becomes a better skater gains an advantage, because he will know how to move without the ball, how to pass, and how to find the open teammate. And in a nutshell, that's the essence of this game.

—Tom LaGarde, NIBBL Founder and Commissioner

Court Specifications

Games are played full-court on a regulation 90-by 50-foot basketball court (wood, concrete, or asphalt). The net is the standard 10 feet high, but it's important that it has at least 5 feet of clearance behind it so players have room to stop or maneuver after a lay-up.

The Game

League matches are played by five-player teams (with one substitute) in four 10-minute quarters, for a total of 40 minutes. The clock stops for free-throws, fouls, injuries, time-outs, and retrieval of the ball when it's so far out of bounds it delays the game. It does not stop for violations or scored baskets except during the last 2 minutes of the game. Each team is allowed three 90-second time outs. Unlimited substitutions are allowed during the game without stopping play. Games start with a jump-ball at center court; at the start of the second half the ball is in the hands of the team that lost the starting jump-ball. Passive zone defenses are not allowed. Teams may play a zone only if it is a zone press; otherwise, defense is strictly player to player. The defensive team can immediately advance the ball after the other team scores, without taking the ball out of bounds first.

Scoring, Fouls, Penalties, and Violations

A field goal nets 2 points, a basket made from beyond an arc 19 feet from the basket (the 3-point line) nets 3, and a basket made from beyond the

25-foot arc nets 4 points. If a shooter is fouled and makes the basket anyway, an extra point is added. A single free-throw is awarded only after a technical foul (when the fouling team is in a penalty situa-

Johan Jansen

Americans versus Netherlanders in Amsterdam.

tion) or if the shooter is fouled in the final 2 minutes of the game. A successful free-throw could be worth 2, 3, or 4 points depending on the distance the fouled player was shooting from. In other words, a player fouled while shooting a 4-pointer is awarded 4 points if she converts the free throw. A nonshooting foul is always awarded 2 points.

There are three types of fouls: player, team, and technical. Player fouls include holding, tackling, or hacking other players. A player is removed after committing six fouls. A team is allowed five team fouls in a quarter. After the fifth (and each subsequent) team foul, the fouling team is considered in penalty and the other team is awarded a free-throw. A technical foul is called for any rough and dangerous play or unsporting conduct. A player committing two technical fouls is removed from the game. After a foul, the referee must touch the ball before it can be put into play; the opposing team then gets a free-throw and possession of the ball.

Palming the ball, double-dribbling, out-of-bounds, and traveling are typical violations. After a violation, the team awarded the ball can put it back into play immediately without the referee having to touch the ball.

Gear

Team members play in standard in-line skates (conventional quads aren't allowed in league play) and helmets. Although checking is prohibited and jumping is not a major component of the game, some players wear knee and elbow pads. Wrist guards are rare because they limit shooting and dribbling, but a pair of bike gloves will protect the palms. The game is played with a standard basketball.

Key Skills

- For defense and advancing the ball, work on backward skating, backward and forward crossovers in both directions, and the ability to make quick directional changes.

- Get used to dribbling the ball while skating fast across the court.

- For more accurate shooting, you need the ability to cut your speed using a heel brake, T-stop, or snowplow to prepare to shoot.

- Jump shots are not required but—as difficult as it is to launch into the air from a wheeled toe—they're becoming more common among experienced players. It doesn't hurt to practice if you feel ready!

- Learn to do a skating lay-up: Approach the net fast, brake, and cross under the basket as you toss the ball up and in.

ROLLER BASKETBALL RESOURCES

National Inline Basketball League (NIBBL)
Tom LaGarde, Commissioner
135 Rivington St., Suite 3F
New York NY 10002
212-539-1132 or 888-GO-NIBBL/
    888-466-4225
fax 212-982-2377
E-mail: nibbl@interport.net
www.nibbl.com

More Resources for Advanced In-Line Skaters

The following list of resources is more general than the sport-specific individual chapter listings, but no less valuable to those seeking additional information about the sport of in-line skating.

In-Line "Portals" on the Web

<www.activeusa.com> An online outdoor recreation magazine with skate-related articles and regional event directories.

<www.getrolling.com> Home of Liz Miller's Get Rolling ORBIT newsletter and website dedicated to in-line fun, fitness, and safety.

<www.in-lineskating.about.com> In-line guide Kathie Fry helps you to "find/learn/share" using an extensive list of links.

<www.n2in-line.com> A virtual community for in-line skaters.

<www.skatecity.com> Skating the Infobahn: Over 1,800 links to in-line skating, quad skating, speed skating, and roller hockey websites.

<www.skategrrl.com> An index to in-line skating websites.

<www.skating.com> This skater's online magazine includes news, instruction, and lots of links.

Trade Associations

International Inline Skating
   Association (IISA), Headquarters
201 N. Front St., #306
Wilmington NC 28401
Kalinda Mathis, Executive Director
910-762-7004, fax 910-762-9744
E-mail: director@iisa.org
www.iisa.org
An industry organization (nonprofit) formed to promote all aspects of in-line skating.

IISA Government Relations
   Committee
201 N. Front St. #306
Wilmington NC 28401
Dave Cooper, Director
313-594-2323
E-mail: iisagr@aol.com
www.iisa.org
Protects skater access rights nationwide.

IISA, National Skate Patrol Division
201 N. Front St., #306
Wilmington NC 28401
Rick Short, NSP National
   Coordinator
301-942-9770
E-mail: 72714.2402@
   compuserve.com
www.iisa.org
A community-based program certifying patrollers to provide instruction, safety tips, and first aid.

IISA/ICP Inline Certification
   Program
P.O. Box 18309
Cleveland Heights OH 44118
Kris Simeone, Director
216-371-2977, fax 216-371-6270
E-mail: icpinline@aol.com
www.iisa.org/icp
The IISA's instructor certification

group; also connects skaters with a local instructor.

National Sporting Goods
   Association (NSGA)
1699 Wall St.
Mount Prospect IL 60056
847-439-4000, fax 847-439-0111
E-mail: nsga1699@aol.com
www.nsgachicagoshow.com
Sporting goods association that puts on trade shows and reports on in-line trends and statistics for the benefit of retailers.

Roller Skating Associations (RSA)
6905 Corporate Dr.
Indianapolis IN 46278
317-347-2626, fax 317-347-2636
E-mail: rsa@oninternet.com

www.rollerskating.org
Membership organization that supports skating rink owners.

Sporting Goods Manufacturers
   Association (SGMA)
200 Castlewood Dr.
North Palm Beach FL 33418
561-842-4100, fax 561-863-8984
E-mail: sgma@ix.netcom.com
www.sportlink.com
Sporting goods trade association working to increase sports participation; presents two product Super Shows each year.

Trail Advocates

Rails-to-Trails Conservancy
   National Headquarters
1100 17th St. NW, 10th Floor

Washington DC 20036
202-331-9696, fax 202-331-9680
E-mail: RTCMail@Transact.org
www.railtrails.org
A nonprofit organization devoted to converting abandoned rail corridors into multiuse trails.

Transportation Equity Act for the
   21st Century (TEA-21)
c/o Surface Transportation
   Policy Project
1100 17th St. NW, Tenth Floor
Washington DC 20036
202-466-2636, fax 202-466-2247
Reauthorizes the landmark 1991 Intermodal Surface Transportation Efficiency Act (ISTEA) to provide government money for trail expansion and enhancements.

■ Index ■

▪ ABOUT THE AUTHOR ▪

Off skates, Liz Miller, an ICP-certified instructor, works as a contract technical writer in northern California. Her favorite forms of rolling are skate-to-ski, fitness, and touring. She guides in-line tourists and gets others rolling through lessons and clinics throughout spring, summer, and fall.

Liz wrote and self-published the first edition of *Get Rolling: The Beginner's Guide to In-Line Skating* in 1992, because no such resource was available to novice skaters at the time. In her second book, *California In-Line Skating: The Complete Guide to the Best Places to Skate,* she rated and described the 300 best tours in her home state. She also contributed the in-line chapter for the 12th edition of *Sports and Recreational Activities,* a college textbook. Other writings include articles for various outdoors publications, including *Northern California Hockey and Skating, Bay Area Parent, Fitness and Speed Skating Times,* and *New York Outdoors.* On the Internet, Liz has written about tours for Thrive Partners' outdoor recreation Go Guide, contributed to the e-zine Skating.com, and publishes her own quarterly ORBIT newsletter at *<www.getrolling.com>.*